PRIVATE GARDENS
of the FASHION WORLD

PRIVATE GARDENS
of the FASHION WORLD

Francis Dorléans

Photography by Claire De Virieu

Introduction by Gabrielle Van Zuylen

Project Director
César Garçon/Inside

ABBEVILLE/VENDOME

NEW YORK

Library of Congress Cataloging-in-Publication Data
is available upon request from the publishers.

First Edition
10 9 8 7 6 5 4 3 2 1

Designed by Marc Walter
Typesetting: Florence Cailly/Hervé Droin
Captions: Jérôme Goutier, translated by Shirley Carse
Coordination: Sabine Greenberg

Contents

*T*he famous couturiers of this century have replaced the Renaissance princes and popes, the kings and nobles of France, the great landowners of the English eighteenth century, the rich of the Industrial Revolution and bankers and mill owners as the innovators and the inventors of form and taste across the world. These men and women come from different countries, different continents, and their influence and vision transforms the lives of all, rich and poor, around the globe. Their eye for line and for life scans, interprets, and forms the world that we work and live in. They fundamentally influence and shape the way we dress, live, and move, and how we see ourselves in time. How logical that their own gardens reveal the sense of their vision–their private world.

The great couturier Cristobal Balenciaga gave his credo after his retirement: "A dress designer must be an architect for the plans, a sculptor for the form, a painter for color, a musician for harmony, and a philosopher to understand measure." His definition of creativity, severely observed during his years of work and crystallized by his reputation, shaped the major figures of today's high fashion. His vision is equally valid for the practice of the art of the garden. The dress designer's art ideally reveals the beauty of the body, its line and movement, in exactly the same way that a great gardener uses the inherent natural possibilities of a site to reveal the beauty of the surrounding landscape.

Hubert de Givenchy speaks for all his colleagues when he states that, "Each article of clothing must become one with every gesture: it's one's life, it is life. Each material is alive." He could be speaking of his gardens, of all gardens. The texture of plants and the architecture of trees are the stuff of all gardens. Color in the garden is the link between the green and brown of the earth and the endless changes of the light in the sky. So what could be more revealing, personal, and fascinating than to see the private gardens of these princes of invention and taste here brilliantly photographed by Claire de Virieu?

Giorgio Armani on the Italian Isola de Pantelleria intensifies the blues of sky and water with an opulence of light and form. Stephan Janson in Tangier uses these elements for a different purpose, while Yves Saint Laurent and Pierre Bergé preserve and intensify the Majorelle garden of Marrakech. In England, Hardy Amies, the Queen's couturier, has created a cottage garden in a village lost in time, while Anouska Hempel's black swans symbolize the strict strength of plan.

In America, Bill Blass has surrounded his eighteenth-century Connecticut house with gardens displaying refinement, elegance, and simplicity. Oscar de la Renta has made a garden of love and memory with his wife Annette beside a magnificent New England landscape. And Kenzo has created a Japanese flower and serenity garden in the Bastille neighborhood in Paris.

To quote Marcel Proust, "By adding here and there a supplementary leaf, I build my work, I dare not say ambitiously like a cathedral, but very simply like a dress."

Gabrielle Van Zuylen

Hardy Amies

The Roses

of the Royal

Couturier

Hardy Amies, now over ninety (opposite), still exhibits a youthful vigor and British sense of style. Like many Englishmen, he is a devoted gardener, and has planted over 160 varieties of roses in the small garden of his Gloucestershire property. A clematis (above) unfolds its large pinkish white double flowers.

"By appointment to Her Majesty the Queen": if anyone has the right to these words on his letterhead, it is Hardy Amies. He has been dressing the Queen of England for forty-two years in accordance with the dictates of the Crown. Forty-two years of turquoise, bright blue, acid green, shocking pink, and canary yellow are proof enough of his constant loyalty and humble submission to the conditions incumbent upon the Queen by virtue of her numerous public duties. She must attend to her subjects and they must be able to recognize her from a distance by the strident colors that she wears. Amies, couturier to the upper classes, has always ignored the noisy clamoring of the media, and puts the demands of his clients' lifestyle before those of fashion. This preference is also reflected in gardening and the country lifestyle bequeathed to the English upper classes by their feudal past: living on one's estate, seeing to one's lands, animals, and gardens. Amies himself would not dream of spending his weekend anywhere other than Gloucestershire, where he owns the most heavenly cottage in Langford, the village that time forgot. There might be the odd car or bicycle to remind visitors that they are not in the mid-nineteenth century, but absolutely nothing seems to

Preceding pages:
The walls of the stone
pavilion and the
property's high enclosing
walls provide surfaces for
a profusion of climbing
roses and honeysuckle.
The centerpiece of the
garden, which was once
the playground of a
country school, is a series
of boxwood borders
framing a cottage garden
(above) of ornamental
tobacco, lavender, and
roses.

have changed since World War II, least of all the little houses groaning under the weight of flowers.

Amies's cottage is in the center of the village, exactly where you would expect to find the village school, which is what his home once was. The garden now occupies the former playground, and even today Hardy Amies is grateful that the town council never had the funds to surface it with tarmac, as is generally the case. "My sister already lived here," he explains. "It was her idea that I should come and take a look at the school when it came up for sale. I bought it immediately, and now I spend every weekend here. It's really supposed to be a weekend cottage, but at my age I think I've earned the right to prolong my weekends, so in fact I'm here much of the week." Amies especially wanted the house to be practical, and treats the garden as a natural extension, "a room like any other room," he says.

Although he is fashion designer to Her Majesty the Queen and is generally considered one of the world's best-dressed men, still nothing can

prepare one for the elegance personified in Hardy Amies. The village may smack of picture postcard, but Amies is the living embodiment of a British look that came in with Beau Brummell and has remained a standard of perfection ever since. Everything is of a piece, from shoes with silk laces to lightly starched shirt, from the impeccably discrete tie to the tailored Harris tweed jacket. If the height of elegance is not to draw too much attention to oneself, then Amies is elegance itself. The way he dresses seems designed to blend with the landscape, so much so that his garden could be the flower he was careful not to put in his but-tonhole, as if his roses would do the job just as well.

Amies's garden was bound to be like him. A landscape designer wasn't needed because the garden is so small, but he does have a gardener—at the age of ninety his days as a manual laborer are over. He admits that he knows a lot about small gardens, but flatly denies that anything he has done here could be called landscape design. He describes his plan as childishly simple. The garden consists mainly of two enormous rectan-

Above: The complementary union of yellow Corydalis lutea *and violet* Campanula portenschlagiana *is set against a box hedge. Following pages: In a four-story garden shed, Amies has artistically grouped small pots of sedum on the top shelves and primroses below, ready to be planted in the spring. This is a beautiful and sumptuous arrangement.*

gular flower beds surrounded by box bushes. "Only the best quality," he insists, as if talking about a piece of fabric. Each flower bed is divided down the middle by a tiny alley, so that the garden is effectively divided into four perfectly equal and symmetrical parts. Amies wouldn't even hear of a lawn—far too time-consuming, particularly when all you really want to do on the weekend is relax. The idea of turning up at a country house to get the lawn mower out was too ghastly to contemplate, particularly considering the dreary racket it makes.

The main alleys are graveled, and Amies sees to it that the gravel is replaced regularly to keep the garden looking its best. The tiny alleys that divide the flower beds are lined with stones, and paved paths run along the feet of the walls on each side of the garden. The different textures of the gravel, stone, and paving slabs in this confined space are among the pleasures of the walk, compounded by the Cotswold stone of the house that closes the perspective. As for flowers, Amies's specialty is

old roses, and while they are in flower one can best understand his garden design. They add a softness made more emphatic by the rather formal symmetry of the overall design. Clouds of roses billow around the front of the house, gathering mainly around the porch and windows, where they immediately plunge the visitor into a bath of petals heavy with scent.

Amies is modest by nature, but he is being slightly provocative when he says that only one hundred and sixty species of roses—nine-tenths of them "old fashioned"—and sixty species of clematis grow along the small walls. So fond is he of roses, he whispers, that he actually owns a second garden in the village. "I surrounded the tennis court with a bed of roses, but since they are only in flower for a short time, I don't go out of my way to ask people to come and see them." This, after all, is a secret garden, and what better words to describe it than the poetic lyrics of Gertrude Stein: "A rose is a rose is a rose . . ."

At the foot of a drystone wall, a rose produces a generous number of semi-double white flowers, and is framed below by a border of trimmed box.

Giorgio Armani

A Volcanic Paradise

Southwest of Sicily,
on the small volcanic
island of Pantelleria,
which was still deserted
twenty years ago, Armani
introduced numerous
plants from the agave
family, such as the Agave
attenuata (above), as well
as hundred-year-old palm
trees brought from the
garden of a palace in
Palermo (opposite).

On this black, stony island, the phosphorescent turquoise blue of the swimming pool sends the elements spinning. The sky and the sea, as if spellbound by this tiny drop of refinement, deepen in intensity—nothing but blue as far as the eye can see. The exquisitely delicate gray of the teak terrace around the pool adds to the impression of refinement. Something about the scene reveals the hand of the designer who created it. This is the island of Pantelleria, an arid outcrop lost at sea between Sicily and Tunisia, and the summer retreat of Giorgio Armani, who is now passionate about a land he was slow to love.

"It was fate that brought me to Pantelleria," says Armani, "I only came to stay with friends. To say it wasn't love at first sight is putting it mildly. I thought the place was wild and dark, almost hostile with its complete lack of vegetation and nothing but rocks for a landscape. It left me cold despite the torrid heat. But gradually I began to see what it had to offer. The sea here is more blue than anywhere else, the air is more pure and heady with fragrance. I fell in love, I suppose, but with that intensity of feeling that comes from loving someone for their faults. I knew I had to come back, so two days before I was due to leave I rushed out and bought a piece of land." The sales negotiation had all the hallmarks of a hurried wedding, nothing too showy and probably all the more likely to succeed because of it.

Preceding pages: *The heat
of a summer's day off
the African coast is fully
felt in this view of
Armani's pool, the curved
deck subtly echoing the
horizon. Water is the
civilizing element of this
near-desert landscape,
and bringing it in
sufficient quantity to
satisfy the needs of many
guests is an accomplishment
on its own.*
Above: *Many ancient
jars can still be found
on Pantelleria; they were
once used for oil and wine,
and serve now as perfect
vehicles for plants in the
garden.*

Armani had just discovered his desert: an ascetic, undeveloped place that would have inspired feelings of peace and concentration in a seventeenth-century mystic. It would be difficult to imagine a place less bucolic than Pantelleria. There is nothing easy about this once-volcanic island with an almost rarefied beauty. At midday, the black earth is positively crushed by the sun, stranded amidst blue tones that know no half measures. When the wind howls, one gets that sense of elation that comes from facing forces greater than one's own.

But light can come from darkness: the immaculate white terraces that Armani has conjured up out of this volcanic rock are like punctuation marks in the lava-like soil of his espaliered garden. The whitewashed walls give a rhythm to the blackened earth, confirming the first impression of a garden more decorative than rustic in design. Cacti naturally deepen this decorative rhythm with their striking shapes.

The abiding impression is of a place wild and bare despite the other plants that Armani has brought in to complement the local flora. He reels off their names with pleasure: "Tiaré trees, magnificent rose bushes, lavender borders, walls of plumbago, hedges of jasmine, and, in particular, trees you wouldn't expect to see in Pantelleria, such as cypress."

In the turbulent life of the designer, this place is restful, but a stay in Pantelleria is not comparable to any conventional seaside holiday. This island is not for the fainthearted. Until the 1960s its name had a ring of misfortune, and it was not until such films as Michelangelo Antonioni's *L'Avventura* and Luchino Visconti's *La Terra Trema* that the world reappraised the beauty of these volcanic islands south of Italy.

Pantelleria is in fact very far south, closer to Tunisia than Italy both geographically and culturally. The geology alone is proof of its origins, when the oceans spewed up molten lava, which has remained resolutely black and resistant to vegetation. During World War II this nearly deserted island came alive as one of Mussolini's many military bases in the Mediterranean. Armani's first move on coming to Pantelleria was to plant an immense palm grove. As he waited for it to grow, he encouraged nature's course by shipping out three hundred-year-old palm trees that he had found growing in a palace in Palermo. Today they make an impressive sight around the pool, particularly at sunset, when they stand silhouetted against a horizon set on fire by the drowning sun. Hearing the wind rattling through the palm trees, it's hard to imagine that twenty years ago this place was totally deserted.

"There was nothing here before," Armani confirms. "I began by buying my first *dammuso* in Cala Levante and went on to buy six other *dammusi* in Gabir, which was originally Arabic and also overlooks the sea"; *dammusi* are little houses of Arab design with slightly rounded roofs and only two rooms. These buildings guarantee each guest a private building and garden. Cala Levante, where the main house is located, has one of the finest views on the island, but until Armani took over only two vines had taken root in the rock surface there. Grapes and capers are the island's only produce, and the locals live off fishing and a traditional white wine that Armani favors.

It is often said that designers are like magicians. The comparison takes on new meaning with Armani, who has succeeded in conjuring a garden out of volcanic land where once it seemed that nothing would grow at all. Armani admits that he didn't do it alone: "I couldn't have supervised the work from where I was living in Milan. And in any case, with the busy life I lead it would have been difficult to complete a project on this scale. That's why I commissioned a Milanese architect, Gabriella Giuntoli, to design both the houses and the terraces. Gabriella, who lives part of the time in Pantelleria anyway and knows it like the back of her hand, made a detailed study of the island's architecture. We got on famously together: I knew what I wanted and Gabriella always knew how to turn what I said into a language that made sense in the context of the place." Of even more vital importance is the vast quantity of infrastructure that was required to install water and electricity and

The black, volcanic soil of Pantelleria can nurture exotic vegetation that needs little rain. In Armani's garden can be found such plants as the Agave victoriae-reginae (left), such cacti as the Cereus peruvianus (center), and many species of cycads (right). Following pages: Armani created a walled terrace from volcanic rock, and planted large and imposing Echinocactus grusonii, which are set off by verdant palm trees and an ever-blue, clear sky. At sunset, this section of the garden is particularly imposing as the setting sun endlessly changes the color of the vegetation.

Only certain plants can pierce the volcanic earth. Aeonium and aloe (above) seem to have succeeded. Palm trees, obviously, thrive in all sorts of desert climates with a minimum of water. Their fruit lends brilliant touches of color: yellow (opposite) and red (above right). These particular plants can be found on one of the terraces Armani created below his house.

establish some of the vegetation. Water in particular is essential not only for plants, but also for guests, who must be able to take all the showers or dips in the pool they need in this heat.

Not before sunset does Pantelleria take on a human face, when the landscape, still panting from the heat of the day, softens and dissolves in the pink vapors of the setting sun. It is at this time that the designer likes to get together with his usually numerous guests. Twenty-five mopeds for their use are proof of his hospitality and the lifestyle he imposes. During the day everyone is free to come and go as they please, but at nightfall they all gather on the terraces overlooking the sea. "I usually spend the month of August on the island, and I like to surround myself with as many friends as possible," Armani says, and friends and the designer share a lively, festive vacation. Armani adores parties and finds that North African folk culture indulges his taste for pageant. With lanterns hanging from trees and carpets, mats, and cushions scattered around, he has all he needs to transform Pantelleria into a land of a thousand and one nights.

Pierre Bergé

The Pursuit of Perfection

Pierre Bergé has reworked the sharply sloping land of his Château Gabriel in Deauville several times in order to create surprises for his many guests. In one area of the garden overlooking the English Channel (following pages) priority has been given to aromatic plants, such wildflowers as mullein, and such domesticated blooms as carnations. The garden is embellished by a bower (opposite) covered in such exuberant vines as clematis (above).

By citing Vicomte Charles de Noailles as the person who initiated him into the joys of gardening, Pierre Bergé acknowledges the very high standard he set for his own endeavors. "Charles de Noailles, a great friend of mine, was a man whose urbanity was of a sort scarcely known today. In him, quite simply, erudition lived in perfect harmony with elegance and charm. Having created at Grasse a garden admired by connoisseurs the world over, Charles took it upon himself to advise me about how to develop a small plot near the Invalides. The project emerged as the first of the gardens that Yves Saint Laurent and I owned together." This was when Bergé conceived a passion for the art of gardens that has never ceased to grow and expand.

Bergé has since perfected his art, producing two gardens in Paris, one in Marrakech, one in Deauville, another in Saint-Rémy, and, most recently, a garden in Tangier. Given this record, one readily believes his declaration that he could not exist without a garden. But in creating so *many* gardens, Bergé has to resign himself to infrequent visits to each; in certain instances, the visits have all but stopped. Still, each of the gardens represents an important moment in his life. And while confessing great admiration for the work done for him by Madison Cox in

Tangier as well as by Michel Semini at Saint-Rémy, Bergé admits that the beauty of the Majorelle garden in Marrakech remains in a class by itself. Bergé's gardening expertise is steeped in theory as well as practice. He learned both from doing and reading, and he knows all the classical writers: Princess Stourza, Prince Wolkonsky, Vicomte de Noailles, Russell Page, Gertrude Jekyll, Sir Edwin Lutyens, and Vita Sackville-West. His thoroughness, taste, and authority played the same crucial role in creating and developing the vast Yves Saint Laurent group, of which he is still president of the couture division. Today if Yves Saint Laurent is the figurehead on the greatest ship of fashion of the second half of the twentieth century, Pierre Bergé is the ship's captain.

On October 30, 1957, Bergé and Saint Laurent were at the funeral of Christian Dior, and their presence there together was pure chance. Saint Laurent was the dauphin of the world's leading fashion designer, and Bergé—a highly reputed art dealer—had known Dior, who had also started out in the same field. Saint Laurent was twenty-one, and Bergé twenty-seven. The highly strung Saint Laurent would soon be drafted into the army, suffer a nervous breakdown, and lose his job at Dior. But Bergé had faith in Saint Laurent's talent, and they became partners in a new fashion house. Their first collection, presented on January 29, 1962, was the biggest sensation since Dior's "New Look" shortly after World War II. Thus began a partnership not only in fash-

Bergé is a great connoisseur of roses, and has devoted an entire garden to them in Deauville: among others to be found there are wild roses (above), or some with very frilly corollas (left).
Opposite: A stone statue seems very much at ease in the midst of grass and weeds, and serves to remind us of the owner's vocation.

Above: The third reincarnation of the walled garden. The first, by Franz Baechler, had medicinal plants, which Louis Benech replaced with vegetables and flowers. Finally Bergé and one of his gardeners created a minimalist, low-maintenance solution of fruit trees, with apple dominating. In spring their brilliant blossoms are well set off by dark pine mulch.

ion, but also in acquiring and redesigning extraordinary houses, collecting art, and being lionized in the intermingled worlds of fashion, art, and society. Bergé, a brilliant businessman, is also highly knowledgeable on the subject of music, and is known for the series of great artists he presented at the Théatre des Champs Elysées and his tenure at the often-troubled New Opéra at the Bastille. Passion goes into his every involvement, from fashion to art collecting, and music to gardening.

When Bergé serves as a guide to the rose garden, the Japanese garden, and the pond on the steep, planted slopes around his Château Gabriel in Deauville, he notes that each holds a surprise. In his other gardens, Bergé enjoyed the aid of a professional landscape designer; the composition of the enclosed garden, however, was his alone, and he was assisted by only one of the gardeners on the property. "All by myself," he repeats several times, vehemently so as to leave no doubts. "Alone with my gardener. Just the two of us—we did the whole thing."

The history of the enclosed garden begins with the talented Swiss

landscapist Franz Baechler, who initiated construction when Bergé and Saint Laurent had him redesign the hundred-acres (forty-hectares) they had recently acquired. The stone walls and corner towers were built at that time on the site of a former tennis court, and Baechler laid out the main axes of the enclosed garden, all of which survive today. Two paths form a cross and, together with other, smaller paths, make up eight identical, square-shaped parterres or flower beds. Within the squares Baechler planted herbs. "Mullein or Aaron's rod, borage, angelica," recites Bergé, who, with a wave of his hand, evokes the numerous other herbs that grew there, the names of which he cannot recall. Gradually, as Baechler's visits became more infrequent, this charming tangle fell into serious disorder. "No doubt there was some negligence on our part," Bergé admits. "I then asked Louis Benech to restore the garden, which he did with all his well-known talent." During this second stage, Benech kept the division of parterres and the straight lines of fruit trees, but introduced a number of aromatic and

The trees are trimmed whenever they get beyond five feet in height, and among the popular varieties found here is the 'Canada Gris' (above), a large and tasty apple, properly labeled in the garden during the spring.

medicinal plants as well as decorative legumes and flowers. He also added a number of wild plants that needed to be controlled and several Mediterranean species requiring considerable attention. All this meant more work for the five gardeners regularly employed on the estate, especially when he decided to redo the enclosed garden once more. Again the plants were uprooted, this time to be replaced by fruit trees trimmed to a uniform height of just under five feet (one and one-half meters). The resulting garden was somewhat a curiosity; in no way was it an orchard, but rather an ornamental garden composed of fruit trees treated in a decorative manner. In winter, the rigor of the arrangement suggested a clock with its interior mechanism revealed. Bergé retained only the most essential elements of the old garden, having pruned away everything likely to distract the eye. The squares were carpeted in pine bark, so that even in summer, when all that geometry took on a bit of color, the enclosed garden retained its look of a carefully rendered line drawing.

Once he takes possession of a new property, Bergé makes the garden his immediate priority. It is only logical, he feels, to first tackle what will require the longest time to finish.

St-Rémy-de-Provence

At his Théo farmhouse in Saint-Rémy, the garden assumed even greater urgency because none existed. The house was named after the brother of Vincent Van Gogh, after whom the street on which it was built is named. The artist, of course, spent a year at an asylum in Saint-Rémy. The land behind the house boasted as much shade as a stripped field—there wasn't a bush or shrub around which to build a shaded garden. On one side was the Rue Vincent Van Gogh, on the other an open field. Bergé describes the property as a small village house where he enjoys lunching under the grape arbor. That may be true today, but the present level of comfort was only achieved through great labor. A decision to transplant grown trees is not to be taken lightly, but at Saint-Rémy there was no choice. "Beyond a certain age," Bergé jokes, "there are two things one cannot do: plant saplings and purchase young wine." Michel Semini, whom Bergé placed in charge of the garden, belongs to the generation that believes that gardens are no longer to be created for posterity but rather for the fastest possible gratification. "Furthermore, I have no children," adds Bergé.

Bergé is seen (above) in his role of hands-on gardener at his recently purchased house at St.-Rémy-de-Provence. One view of the garden (opposite) shows anthemis, chrysanthemums, and petunias—all of which can enjoy the shade of a large tree—as well as box shaped into spheres and large, stately Provence cypress. It would be difficult to imagine that all this was created quite recently, but Bergé is an extremely busy and active gentleman who does not like to wait.

Everywhere one goes in
Provence is a reminder of
the short, unhappy life of
Vincent van Gogh who
lived and suffered in St.
Rémy. Pierre Bergé's
house is, in fact, named
after the artist's brother
Théo. These two views of
fields could well have been
the inspiration for one of
the master's highly
originally colored
paintings. Lavender lends
a note of color to Bergé's
olive grove (above), and
wild poppies seem like
bright rubies in another
green grove (opposite).

Within twelve months, Semini had created from scratch a Provençal
garden that gives the illusion of having been there forever. The quiet
pleasure found in the Théo garden blots out any memory of the heavy
bulldozers required to accomplish the transformation. The shade now
cooling the garden is as precious to Bergé as a spring welling up in the
desert, especially at high noon, when the sun virtually immobilizes the
surrounding countryside. But here the heat is tempered by the happy
disposition of trees and water, and the allure of the swimming pool
draws guests with the full force of their inertia. It is a beautiful pool,
graced by a simplicity of line that compensates for its somewhat
anachronistic character. It could almost be a Roman bath, an impression aided by a statue of Neptune flanked by amphorae. On either side,
fields of lavender, their intense color burning away under the sun, generate a mirage-like shimmer, discouraging all desire to move.
In this kind of heat the garden seems to dissolve into the countryside. In
reality, however, what makes the garden appear so perfectly integrated

with its environment is the sheer simplicity of the composition. Semini conceived of the site as a succession of rooms, each with decorative surprises. At a cooler time of day, when all manner of unnoticed things come to the fore, up spring such surprises as an aviary, Andalusian vases, and a terra-cotta faun slaking its thirst in a fountain. There is a subtle relationship of color from one end of the garden to the other, as in the dominant green (ranging from the raw verdure of the bamboo trees to the ash grays of sage and olive) that sweeps through and roils the blue waves of lavender, iris, wisteria, and agapanthus. This blue-green monochromy represents nothing more than a clever exploitation of local color, utilizing almost exclusively plants native to the Mediterranean soil. Depending on the season, though, the garden is also enriched with other colors, as when the poppies bloom in the olive grove at the end of the property. "We would have arranged this on purpose had it been possible," Bergé claims. "But growing poppies is a process that still eludes us; only the wind is capable of sowing their seed."

Van Gogh also loved to paint Provence's irises, which magnificently embellish one of Bergé's garden paths in the spring, when the landscape is at its most beautiful (following pages).

Left: *A young stag, carved in stone, seems to be quenching his thirst in a quiet setting, the dominating colors of which are gray and green, which appear in stone, olive trees, boxwood, and sage.*
Below: *A dwarf Pittosporum tobira 'Nana,' is an excellent choice for a magnificent Anduze vase.*
Opposite: *In June the agapanthus are the result of the first heat of summer, bringing a note of color.*

He takes even greater pleasure from all this because it confirms a theory he has often verified: in nature all colors come together and accommodate one another marvelously. Don't talk to Bergé of all-white gardens, a fashion he cannot abide. "White gardens!" he exclaims with upturned eyes, before taking a breath and clarifying his outburst. "I admire white gardens like the one laid out by Vita Sackville-West at Sissinghurst Castle: a white room whose beds of white flowers generate a startling effect at the center of a green park. But all those uniformly white gardens created during the last decade evince nothing so much as a lack of imagination and a tiresome conformity." Bergé is rarely halfhearted in his reactions. By habit, he speaks forthrightly and draws precise, astute conclusions: "Color remains an extraordinary source of inspiration. I could not imagine an artist without colors. What kind of collections would have come from Yves Saint Laurent, a designer who consistently finds inspiration in the splendor of the Majorelle garden, if we had planted nothing but lily of the valley?"

Bill Blass

Living

with History

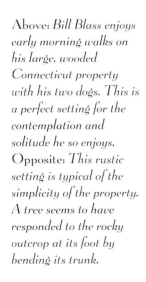

Above: *Bill Blass enjoys early morning walks on his large, wooded Connecticut property with his two dogs. This is a perfect setting for the contemplation and solitude he so enjoys.* Opposite: *This rustic setting is typical of the simplicity of the property. A tree seems to have responded to the rocky outcrop at its foot by bending its trunk.*

Connecticut affords a sense of luxury similar to treading on new carpet—real countryside less than an hour from New York, with a landscape made for privacy without the threat of isolation. It also offers the promise of the American weekend: well-heeled, warmly dressed comfort, with the look and smell of fall and deer scattering in the woods. Rows of white cottages, swimming pools, and clubhouses add the finishing touches to a complete landscape.

The property owned by designer Bill Blass is quite different from most of the other, over-pampered second homes nearby. His is a period house, authentically late-eighteenth-century and solid as a rock. The house is uncompromisingly austere, with a rustic American style. It dates back to the American Revolution, and it reflects an idealized rural society where material needs were not of primary importance. Blass's New York apartment reflects the same principles of order and austerity.

With his large country house the designer also acquired memories—almost a page of history, in fact. George Washington apparently came here to meet with representatives of the British government in a last-ditch attempt to prevent the increasingly likely war with England. That

moment is echoed in the garden, where a contemplative atmosphere is made still deeper by the closeness of the forest into which the garden mysteriously disappears.

The house was built in 1769 as an inn and post house, which explains its two-story structure. According to the sign that once hung outside, it was called the Inn of the Sabbath. It is a tough, solid structure, built entirely of rough-hewn gray stones and rather plain except for a steepish stoop and sash windows opening onto the garden.

Blass is a master of detail, both in his landscaping and his elegant dresses. A traditional picket fence is crafted from logs (left), and a sundial embellishes a verdant flower bed shaded by large trees (below right). Blass's house dates from the end of the eighteenth century, is highly traditional and historic, and was once a tavern (below left).

Today, however, the house's absence of frills gives it a unique elegance, like a stripped, unembellished version of the gray-stoned Trianon at Versailles. The garden achieves the same effect by its dogged refusal to take the path of least resistance. Its refinement is obvious in the extraordinary attention to detail: how the fences have been pegged together, for example; how the low stone walls have been constructed; how the various fields interlock; and how the gnarled tree trunks that grow in them stand out like sculpture.

"Color is distracting," says Blass, who has found this to be generally true in his work. His garden illustrates this principle by the almost exclusive use of green: flowers are few and far between. The only other color seen in abundance is gray, which is found in the stones of the house as well as certain bas-reliefs and other sculptures that are scattered here and there in a sometimes entirely unexpected fashion. In one case, the visitor stumbles across a relief of an early nineteenth-century group entangled in brambles in the woods.

Above: Rather than the old post house, Blass chose as his quarters a small garden cottage, the modest appearance of which blends into the landscape.
Following pages: Sculpture can be found throughout the garden. One of the most original pieces is a raised stone "path of initiation" created by Blass himself as a representation of the thread of Ariadne, really a representation of the development of the spirit.

Opposite: *In the heart of the forest, Blass creates a surprise with this sculptured group dating from the beginning of the nineteenth century.*

Stretching the palette to its limits, the swimming pool is an almost military green and yet enormously refined. It is deliberately out of place and considerably more severe than the typical weekend-home pool. What we call the garden is, in fact, a succession of meadows with occasional flat clumps of foliage acting as barriers between the different levels of the naturally sloping land. Low, gray stone walls are another dominant theme: one in particular traces a strange course through the grass arrousing contemplation. Blass designed it as an allegorical sculpture to represent the course of thought, but it could equally well be the stream of life.

Blass is accustomed to hearing himself described as the doyen of American fashion. In fact, his talents first took him to New York in 1940, shortly after his eighteenth birthday. He studied there briefly, then took his first fashion job as a sketch artist. He enlisted in the Army during World War II, then returned to New York and began his career as a designer. At Anna Miller & Co., before and after that company's merger with Maurice Rentner in 1958, Blass rose from head designer to vice president, and then to owner. 1970 made legal what everyone had known for some time, as the name of the company was changed to Bill Blass Ltd. For decades Blass has presided over the refinement of a taste that became the rage in the 1960s. He was staging fashion shows when American couture was in its infancy and few American designers could compete with their European counterparts. The Blass look centers

Connecticut is heavily wooded, and this abundance is reflected throughout the property and the house itself. A pile of firewood is stacked between trees (top), and a wooden gazebo with a shingle roof provides an enchanting place of rest (above).

around luxury and glamour, but it can also be quite fanciful: his Matisse collection, for example, allowed women to wear a painting, albeit one woven in India.

His longstanding supremacy has brought with it some advantages. Most importantly, he has earned the right to be himself whatever the occasion—a rare privilege indeed. Blass has nothing left to prove; his clothes are worn around the world, and perfumes and licenses say the rest. He originally bought the house in Connecticut as a weekend place, but he now spends at least four days a week there. He takes great advantage of his freedom in the country, walking in the woods with his dogs, far from the hustle and bustle of the city, and particularly far from the crazed attention of the media. Despite his active life in New York, one of his favorite moments is daybreak at his Connecticut house.

Early morning solitude is stolen time, time to think, and in a house so steeped in history, there's no shortage of things to meditate on. When Blass wakes up in the morning, he can almost hear George Washington in negotiations with the English envoys. His bedroom is where the meetingroom once stood. Closing his eyes, he can practically hear the clatter of steel, the slap of leather, the stamping of hooves, noises from the past that rattle through his brain. This is music to charm the ear of any history lover. Outside, the dew-soaked garden that is still blue with night and heavy with sleep shakes itself awake as the sun breaks over the horizon, swathed in wispy ribbons of pink and mauve. As he opens the door of the pantry to let his dogs out, Blass watches them for a moment before turning in silent veneration to the rising sun.

Wood is the dominant note on the property, whether it edges the swimming pool or covers a cabana (opposite); forms the initials of the owner (top); or covers the terrace in front of his house (above).

Loulou de la Falaise

The Muse
of Saint Laurent

In the heart of the Vexin in France, Loulou de la Falaise and her husband, Thaddée Klossowski, conceived this handsome garden of skillfully organized disorder. They have planted many roses and dahlias that bloom for long periods over the summer (above). Thaddée not only fixes things around the house, but also built the tree house (opposite).

"The last house in the village, where the road comes to an end"; this is not only a very useful way of explaining to friends how to get there, but is also a precise description of what Loulou de la Falaise was looking for—a real country house, far from everything but easily accessible, with a big garden that disappears into the woods.

It isn't easy thinking of Loulou de la Falaise as a child of nature. For years she was Yves Saint Laurent's muse and inspiration and, as a result, an international high-fashion icon. She was the personification of the YSL style for her contemporaries and the last word in casual refinement. She was so famous among the young that even those who didn't know her never called her anything other than Loulou. All eyes were on her. She brought a new kind of cultivation to glossy fashion magazines, and in real life she had a singular and provocative style. She caused a sensation wherever she went and she never came home until dawn. Her life had all the glamour of the mythical *femme fatale*, dripping with turbans, fringes, feathers, furs, and, especially, costume jewelry. For Yves Saint Laurent she was the woman who could turn paste into much, much more than the real thing. She was jewelled and dazzling and she still sets his creations on fire.

Above: *De la Falaise greatly enjoys the planned disorder of the daisy garden.*
Below: *The magical flowering of peonies is all too fleeting, but they are rapidly replaced by the blooming of roses and dahlias.*

When the press creates the image of a famous person, it tends to ignore any details that might not fit. In her case, her English countryside childhood was not nearly so interesting to the press as her misspent youth in swinging London, or the fashionable life she led in Paris. Her grandfather was the renowned portraitist Sir Oswald Birley, her mother, Maxine, a fashion editor, but her celebrated marriage to Thaddée Klossowski, son of the painter Balthus, says even more about the fashionable circles in which she moved.

Even today, at her property in the Vexin, north of Paris, de la Falaise thinks it is fate that put her house where the road ends, as if the road had decided to revert to a cart track and had rejected its asphalt right before coming to her house. "Maybe it was because we couldn't go any further," says Loulou. "But as soon as we got there I felt I'd arrived. The minute I stepped in the door, I was home." The garden had been abandoned for years, and was choked with brambles. The house in the middle of the brambles looked like something out of *Sleeping Beauty:* by some miracle it remained just as the eighteenth-century architect had left it, complete with huge French doors that opened onto the garden, which had fared less well, particularly during World War II, when the entire village used it as a place to grow vegetables. "Apparently they'd planted sweet potatoes where the roses were, rutabagas where the wild pansies were, and even the window boxes had been requisitioned for tomato plants."

By the time de la Falaise and her husband Thaddée moved in, any sign of roses or sweet potatoes had long since disappeared with the rest of the garden. They only began to get an idea of what the garden had looked like when the clearing began. The principal axis ran from the manor house to the forest, and Loulou carpeted this path with lawn to give it a softer edge. It now flows through the garden that grows on either side. Every year new plants make the garden more beautiful. The original flowerbeds were too formal for the lady of the house, who has turned them into a wandering pattern, often of tall flowers that form screens: big sunny clumps of solidagos with their yellow plumes; potentillas, irises, dahlias, and Japanese anemones. True to her generation, Loulou worships disorder and delights in the prevailing anarchy in nature. She adores the naturalness of wildflowers, as seen in the inclusion of poppies, daisies, and buttercups in even her most elaborate floral compositions. As she points out, not without some satisfaction, the garden is still "a bit of a mess." And so it should be: she works very hard to keep it that way.

The air of quiet abandon makes the place utterly charming, disheveled, madly romantic. It does rain a lot in the area, but de la Falaise finds this melancholic climate, with its changes of mood and sudden bursts of rain, enchanting. "It's not to everybody's taste," she admits, "but I've remained very English where that's concerned. The countryside for me has got to be wet. You've got to feel water welling up beneath your feet when you walk. You've got to want to put on gumboots. And once you've got them on, you can't wait to go off exploring in the woods to smell that unmistakable wetness, the smell of the earth just after it's rained. It's delicious." This profession of faith also reveals the mood that inspired her to plant willows at the edge of the wood. They recreate the kind of scene sometimes found on the banks of a stream: a Bohemian atmosphere that suits her melancholy soul. She says she needs poetry and mystery like other people need comfort and security.

Loulou had rather lost touch with nature until the birth of her daughter Anna. It was now her daughter's turn to experience everything that

A large lawn in front of the harmoniously proportioned eighteenth-century main house is bordered by a profusion of cactus dahlias that provide a enchanting display of red, white, pink, and orange throughout the summer and autumn.

had made Loulou's own childhood so magical: cutting flintstone, holding grass between your fingers and making it whistle, picking berries in the woods, snakes slithering through the long grass, startled rabbits leaping out, poisonous toadstools with red-and-white dotted caps, and discovering slimy slug trails and acrobatic spiders. Her voice becomes croaky when she recalls the tree house that Thaddée built for their daughter: "It was the prettiest tree house that any little girl might dream of. It was only after we studied the plans that we realized that the tree in question belonged to our neighbor. Fortunately by then Anna had got to an age when children lose interest in tree houses."

Muses, as everyone knows, are placed on pedestals. But seeing Loulou bent over a shovel, her hands and fingernails caked in dirt, one wonders on just what kind of pedestal she belongs. It's certainly easier to imagine her playing with precious stones than pulling up weeds. "For a muse, I use a lot of energy," she jokes. Ultimately, she sees little difference between picking up snail shells and choosing fine gems, which is not surprising from someone who once had gravel made especially to suit a particular design. She has always said that she prefers stones that look like pebbles. "I couldn't begin to define inspiration," she admits, "but I know it always takes you by surprise." Some words, some colors, she says, have the power to unlock her imagination for reasons that she can't explain. She is often unsure what inspired her to create a piece of jewelry. It might have been the sun's reflection in a leaf or the shape of a stem blowing in the wind. "The truth is that I'm yours for a handful of brightly colored trinkets and a few well chosen words."

Opposite: *One area of the garden has become a flower meadow where daisies and buttercups mix quite naturally with the delicate light-pink flowers of the large perennial poppy, 'Prinzessin Victoria Louise.'*
Above: *A riot of color, as well as delightful forms, is created by the giant spikes of delphiniums in the midst of tall grass and daisies.*

Ferragamo-di San Giuliano

The Leopard's Garden

Above: *The Marchese di San Giuliano continues his memories of his late wife, Fiamma Ferragamo, by maintaining this marvelous exotic garden in eastern Sicily. The house and its adjoining chapel present a seventeenth-century facade worthy of the Italian Baroque.* Opposite: *In the shadow of a stone pine grow numerous cacti, which can be enjoyed from the main terrace of the house.*

The Marchese di San Giuliano has never before allowed his garden to be photographed. It's a private place, and the tranquility of the garden has never suffered, according to him, by being kept from the curiosity of the public. He only agreed to change his mind as a memorial to his late wife Fiamma, who passed away two years ago following a long illness. Fiamma was the oldest of the six children of Salvatore Ferragamo, who was the first shoemaker to inscribe his name on the world of fashion. The name has since become a legend that Fiamma—who succeeded her father as head of the department that produced the beautiful shoes— spent her entire life developing. As the eldest child, she had the good fortune to learn the trade during her father's lifetime. She was sixteen when she started; he died one year later. While waiting for her six brothers and sisters to join her, she was the first link in the chain that preserved the family's direction of Ferragamo during its international expansion. As a testimony, her husband wanted her memory to flower in one of these chapters devoted to designers' gardens. He is what is known as a *grand seigneur*, and the living embodiment of Giuseppe Tomaso di Lampedusa's novel *The Leopard*. Very elegant in a green loden coat thrown over his shoulders, the Marchese could easily have played the

role of the Prince of Salina in the Luchino Visconti film adaptation of the book. He is the same age, and is broadly enough built to play the lion-like hero. As he pays homage to the autumn sun, the golden stubble of the fall harvests has turned the fields into the smooth pelt of a wild cat, spotted with stunted tree trunks and stones. Though some hastily constructed buildings disfigure the coast road, the land in the interior has changed little since the Risorgimento, which brought the Kingdom of Naples and Two Sicilies into the bosom of Italy.

The property known as San Giuliano, which is approached by miles of zigzagging roads through orange groves, has been in the marchese's family for eight or nine centuries. The villa is difficult to date, but it must go back to at least the fifteenth or sixteenth century. Flanked on one side by a chapel, this solid building defies estimates. It was originally a fortified farm, as a remnant of battlements reveals. It would still have a severe appearance without the young vines that breach the austerity of the architecture by bathing several parts of the facade in a green tide that moves with the slightest wind. The delicate color of the old walls is also unmilitary: an exquisite old rose color bordering on gray, and unobtainable anywhere else, since it is made by grinding up small stones from the nearly extinct crater of Mount Etna. The long buildings of the common area enclose the first courtyard, which is shaded by an enormous ficus. With its creepers and roots inextricably interlinked, this forms a near forest on its own. The was the first tree the marchese planted when he returned from Brazil in 1959. He was forty-one years old. A border of prickly plants and cacti in front of one of the buildings orients the visitor to the nature of the garden.

The years of his youth spent in Brazil certainly contributed to his fondness for this tropical style. Seven years there and nearly three in the Bahamas, where he worked for Olivetti, made him familiar with this sort of vegetation, which he attempted to acclimatize to his own land when he returned home. The Sicilian sun favored these experiments, and success was soon achieved. San Giuliano lavished them with care, making them even more resistant and solid than they had been in their own habitat. The marchese, however, credits the microclimate here, caused by a warm current that passes over the Sicilian coast. Despite his modesty, the forty species of palm tree alone testify to the effect of his devotion. Fiamma used to jokingly complain that he spent more time on his plants than his family.

The grandeur of Sicily's past, as well as the importance of the San Giuliano family, are evident in a fountain (opposite) *that the present marchese moved from a nearby village to his garden; it bears the family's coat of arms. Two oleanders flourish in what was once the font. Bougainvillea are rampant in the warm, dry Sicilian climate, and a splendid example has been planted in an antique, earthenware vessel* (above).
Following pages: *San Giuliano brought exotic plants from around the world for his garden, and patiently acclimatized them. Here is a profusion of yuccas, notably* Yucca elephantipes, *enlivened by low tufts of cycads.*

The garden boasts an extraordinary richness of flowers from all climates. The decorative leaves of a lotus plant begin to unfurl prior to summer flowering, when it produces a pronounced scent of almonds (left). The garden is perfumed throughout the summer by a profusion of datura (right).

The flora of deserts from all over the world now grow on the immense lawn in front of the villa. Some of the plants come from North American canyons, others from the African bush, Australia, or Guadeloupe, and a number come from Brazil and other parts of South America. Most were given to him by friends, and the marchese considers his garden a sign of friendship, though the way he speaks of his plants reveals love. The passion that annoyed the marchesa during her lifetime has now also become a way for her husband to rediscover and keep alive her memory.

No one before the marchese had thought of organizing a pleasure garden around the villa, mainly because the property was never before considered a vacation house. It was a farm of vegetables and fruit that made up a seemingly endless Garden of the Hesperides at a time when golden oranges were the principal economic support of Sicily. Used to dealing in thousands of acres, the San Giuliano family didn't even know the exact amount of acreage they owned in lands stretching all the way to Syracuse. Today nearly a thousand acres (four hundred hectares) are

devoted to citrus fruit, giving rise to fulminating activity in the kitchens of the villa, where syrups, jams, and candied peels are prepared. In the spirit of enterprise inherited from her father, Fiamma marketed the recipes that had been handed down from generation to generation of her husband's family. Though it began as a hobby, it has become an industry, and today one finds San Giuliano jam as far away as Tokyo. The marchese's description of his wife bent over enormous boiling cauldrons evokes an alchemist trying to create gold from a base metal. The golden brew of orange peel obeyed Fiamma's instructions as she filled thousands of jars of marmalade each year.

Encouraged by the success of his first garden, the marchese recently decided to create a second, more sophisticated one. Enclosed by walls, it is framed by canals and ditches in the fashion of an Islamic garden. The overflow of basins on the edge creates a splashing sound that summons coolness, while benches against the walls allow the visitor to enjoy the serenity of the place. These benches are covered in tiles, which also

Sicily is famous for its fruit. As citrus predominate, a profusion of plums (above) present an almost exotic appearance.

Right: *San
Giuliano recently created
a new garden at the
bottom of his property.
Enclosed by walls, this
Islamic retreat has lovely
benches covered in tiles,
which have also been used
as paving. The garden
has been divided into four
sections, and has a
fabulous view of
Mt. Etna.*

Opposite: *Among the
exotic plants brought to
the garden by its owner is
Parkinsonia aculeata, a
large Mexican bush with
prickly branches that can
even ensnare birds.*
Below: *The slow-
growing* Chorizia
speciosa *has a very
bumpy and thorny trunk.*

From the same family as the arum lily, elephant ears (or giant taro), Alocasia macrorrhiza, require a great amount of water and heat to display the large and admirably structured leaves (above) and their strange spadices (right).
Opposite: *After watering, bamboo canes make a lovely impression.*

unfurl like a carpet on the ground. In the center of the two paths that divide the garden into four sections is a Baroque fountain found by the marchese at a local dealer. One garden of aromatic herbs, one of olive and grapefruit trees, and two of tropical plants make up the four parterres. The principal path is shaded by a bower of forty different species of grapes. Cypresses add to this composition, which also displays a view along the path onto Mount Etna in the distance, crowned with vine leaves like a god of antiquity.

The extraordinary beauty of this timeless vision brings us back again to Lampedusa's masterpiece. "We were leopards, lions . . . we will replace jackals and hyenas. But all leopards, lions, jackals, sheep will continue to take us as the salt of the earth," foresees the Prince of Salina, adding, "That shouldn't be able to last, but it will last forever. The human 'forever:' a century or two." The end does not seem to have come, and the garden of the Marchese di San Giuliano leads us to believe that Sicily still has several reasons to take itself for the salt of the earth.

John Galliano

The Rose

Tattoo

Above: *John Galliano* (left) *imposed the choice of roses, and talented landscape artist Camille Müller* (right) *transmitted to the designer his own passion for bamboo and highly structured plants like acanthus, with its large white spikes.*
Opposite: *The perfect understanding between Galliano and Müller was born in the cleverly organized disorder of Galliano's jungle-like Paris garden.*

Decadent, divine, and resistant to bourgeois convention in all its forms, John Galliano stubbornly remains uncorrupted by success. He is the wildest of all the couturiers, and the timely *fin-de-siècle* label he earned at his debut is still consistent with his rather outrageous brand of sophistication. While Galliano's name may now be closely associated with that of Christian Dior, the English-born designer still retains his own couture house, first established in the Bastille quarter (provisionally, as it turned out, owing to the want of space). When it became possible for him to move to a smarter neighborhood, Galliano chose the Rue d'Avron near the Place de la Nation, far from such traditional couture streets as the Boulevard Saint-Germain or the Avenue Montaigne. Here he found plenty of room in a three-story, former toy factory. In terms of prestige, however, the site left something to be desired. The Rue d'Avron led to the flea market from the Porte de Montreuil, which not too long ago marked the beginning of Paris's northern slum. Today the slum is gone, but the quarter continues to be a thing apart, the old proletariat having been replaced by immigrant workers from every corner of the globe. Lively as the area may be, it is scarcely a place where one would expect to find a couture house—not to mention a couturier's garden.

Garden designer Camille Müller thought of something wholly unexpected there, as well, in a vision of a rose tattooed on a shoulder. This image sprang from the dismay and wonder he felt in the just-discovered domain of John Galliano. A week earlier, Müller had known virtually nothing about the fashion world. Before accepting the commission for the garden, he first visited the site in the early hours of the day to ensure a first impression free of outside influences. On his visit to Galliano's building, he had been thinking of a flower, and a rose tattoo had taken shape in his mind, a flower superimposed on the abandoned terrain before him. He understood immediately why Galliano was seduced by the building. On the freshly restored facade, the brickwork alternated in tonality between sand and ocher, while the windows, transformed into glass-filled bays, endowed the nineteenth-century structure with a spidery lightness. The garden was another matter: neglected for a decade, the site was now little more than a vacant lot. It made a poor framework for the extremely sophisticated style practiced by the young Galliano, whose daring had made him the talk of the town.

Finding a way to bridge the gap between that sophistication and the relatively modest proportions of the space before him presented a daunting, albeit exciting, challenge. The Baroque world of John Galliano defied easy translation into horticulture. Also to be considered was the urge to escape the present in every one of the designer's shows. Müller uncovered the remains of a stone-paved courtyard in front of the brick edifice, while amid the dense brushwood stood a wild willow tree and a cherry laurel of impressive size. With his practiced eye, Müller had already spotted the few shrubs worth saving, when suddenly a great commotion signaled Galliano's arrival. For the last week the garden designer had heard so many contradictory things about the couturier that he no longer knew what to expect. Yet all apprehension vanished once Müller found himself in the presence of the man himself.

Not only did Müller find Galliano sympathetic, he even felt drawn to him by a current of understanding, divining that the sensibility of the designer accorded with his own. Within Galliano's manner, and its dandified excesses, he sensed a touching vulnerability. The two men got along as kindred spirits and, above all, as complements of one another. While Müller knew nothing about couture, Galliano had little grasp of botany. Just as work began, Galliano realized that he owned a book about Müller, a volume he had looked through not long before. Galliano

Opposite: *The surfinia, a petunia with an improved bloom, falls elegantly over a garden chair that serves as its support.*
Above: *At the base of the bamboo, Müller opted for a profusion of flowers, among them the prolific campanulas with large violet and pale pink bells.*

Thanks to the protection from the elements offered by nearby buildings, bamboo has grown nearly thirty-five feet (eleven meters) high in Galliano's garden. It makes a perfect foil for several flowers that have been planted among it, including such climbing roses as an apricot-yellow variety with double petals (left and below), and large hydrangeas *(opposite).*

feels that this bit of reading afforded a premonition of things to come. Each of the gardens in the book, while preserving an offhanded, but quite individual charm, told a different story, and Galliano loves stories. He confided to Müller that he liked roses: perfumed, in cascades, bushes, or bowers. The wild romanticism that lurked beneath this passion was certainly consistent with the nature of the artist. It also evoked Galliano's nationality, and Müller visualized several enclosures dedicated to English roses, the delicate flesh tones of which would bring warmth to the rose tattoo.

First, however, Müller had to solve several difficult technical problems.

Above: *A foxglove with pale pink flowers and a clear pink rose make a lovely pair before a densely verdant background.*
Opposite: *The considerable height of newly planted bamboo already obscure the lovely renovated facade. Along the length of the paved path, acanthus show off their handsome evergreen leaves, superbly serrated and decorative year-round.*

To finish off a huge, half-buried air-conditioner and yet leave it accessible, he crowned the machine with a nineteenth-century style, wrought-iron gazebo. A fair amount of earth had to be moved, a millstone wall constructed to buttress the upper part of the garden, rocks brought in for the fountain, and cobblestones laid to allow for turning the soil. In the Parisian climate, anything that grows higher than surrounding walls risks freezing in the winter. But thanks to the great height of the neighboring buildings, bamboo has grown as tall as thirty-five feet (eleven meters). Their golden stalks stand against the wall like a verdant screen creating the illusion of light.

Today the garden exudes an air of nonchalance, however deceptive. In reality, almost nothing is left to chance, even in the cleverly organized and maintained disorder animating the borders. Here a fence supports the bulky, cascading clusters of a climbing rose; there a trellis hedge unleashes the dizzy profusion of an anthemis grove; while farther along a wrought-iron chair accommodates a burst of Parma flowers and violets. A stone path leads to a flight of wooden steps and provides a means of touring the garden from one end to the other. Sandy infill allowed moss to spring up quickly in the network of cracks between the paving stones, which thus lose their harsh look and feel. They unroll like a carpet even as they function as a path, and the little semicircular area that fans out before the building resembles a clearing in the woods. The pots filled with boxwood, trimmed into spheres, both mark off the space and bring a degree of order to the riot of flowers. The roses (some varieties of which renew their blooming throughout the season) command a great deal of attention. Foxgloves and bellflowers, thrusting up on their stalks, attempt to rival the height of the bamboo, superbly indifferent to the currants and raspberries growing around their feet. The latter, meanwhile, bear witness to the decorative potential of edible plants.

In the second part of the garden, where Galliano likes to take tea, the serried ranks of bamboo form a vault of foliage. Once recovered from their surprise and accustomed to the muted light, visitors discover a fountain surmounted by a laughing Buddha, a sculpture brought back from Bali. A banana tree completes the sense of an improvised jungle, while hanging Venetian lanterns add a touch of Baroque to the general atmosphere of makeshift exoticism. In sum, this is a garden bearing the stamp of couture that manages to make the disorder of nature resemble the messy, tumbling tresses of this couturier decked out in lace and baubles.

Hubert de Givenchy

Perfection in Three Gardens

Above: *Hubert de Givenchy owns three gardens, the largest of which is at his eighteenth-century château at Jonchet in the Eure-et-Loire district near Paris. Its facade displays a classicism worthy of the distinguished designer. In winter, snow highlights the banks of the moat* (opposite), *as well as the carefully thought-out geometry of the formal garden's plan* (following pages).

Rhododendrons parading through a succession of *Régence* salons paneled in white and gilt is not something you see every day. This strange convoy inched its way across the inlaid parquet floor of the two immense rooms that lead to Hubert de Givenchy's Paris garden. Unlike the furniture, which had been removed the day before, the crystal chandeliers remained, and seemed to court disaster. The rhododendrons occupied the room like a thousand pink candles, filling the air with a sound like the noisy rustling of crinolines. A bull in a china shop is the image that immediately springs to mind, but even though the plants in transit may have been the size of elephants, they were also as fragile as porcelain.

Transplanting trees more than thirteen feet (four meters) high is always a challenge, and Givenchy hesitated for some time. Today he congratulates himself on what he admits was a crazy idea. The French doors of the salon open on to a large lawn bordered with foliage now bustling with flowering rhododendrons. They light up the garden with that touch of refinement expected from haute couture. This should come as no surprise: for more than forty years, Givenchy has been a credit to his profession. The prodigious talent that he has displayed throughout his career is on the

Seen here is the formal garden in two seasons. In winter (above) the geometry is emphasized, while in the summer (opposite) a luscious green predominates in box borders, grass and foliage. The design was inspired by plans Givenchy discovered at the Church of San Giorgio Maggiore in Venice. Thirty-six thousand box plants were used to create an astonishingly modern and geometric image.

same scale as his physique: at six foot four inches, Hubert de Givenchy towers above his peers, who tend to be on the small side. He is not only a great couturier, but also a great gentleman, one of a vanishing breed whose honesty and decency put them well above the norm.

"You have to be either innocent or very rich to open a couture house," Givenchy said when he showed his first collections in 1952. He claims that he was innocent, and since it is written that the meek shall inherit the earth, he never looked back. His clients included such famous ladies as Jackie Kennedy, the Duchess of Windsor, Gloria Guiness, Mona Bismark, Princess Grace, and Marella Agnelli. Audrey Hepburn was another client, but more than that she was also a friend and inspiration. The now-legendary story of their first meeting remains one of the most charming anecdotes in the history of fashion. They lived happily ever after, beautifully dressed, and saw their talents combined in a great many children: *Sabrina, Funny Face, Love in the Afternoon, Charade, How to Steal a Million Dollars,* and the sublime *Breakfast at Tiffany's.*

Givenchy today says haute couture is a thing of the past. What does he think of his successors and of fashion today? "It's not the same anymore," is his rather terse response. "What you see around you now has nothing in common with haute couture as I understood it and made it." Only when he talks about his three gardens (one in Paris, Le Jonchet in Eure-et-Loir, and the Clos Fiorentina in Cap Ferrat) is he once again the great designer. He is attentive to the smallest detail, and can describe a flower arrangement as lovingly as a hat. Taste rarely covers everything—to love painting is not to know about music; a person who dresses beautifully may not know about interior design or how to set a table. "And yet, it is all part of the same thing," says Givenchy. "Couture is a close relative of interior design, which is itself not unrelated to gardening." As further proof of the inter-relatedness of these fields, Givenchy today is president of the supervisory board at Christie's, and insists they twisted his arm to take the job. But after forty years dedicated to couture, it amuses him to do something different.

A charming old pavilion
(above and opposite) in
the kitchen garden is used
to store garden furniture,
while the tool shed
(below) was inspired by
similar follies in the
United States, including
the weathervane.

It's easy to see why the art of gardening is not for everyone, but Givenchy is as comfortable here as he is in couture. His upbringing makes him extremely modest, and the only thing of which he boasts is having been well taught. He says that he owes everything as a couturier to Balenciaga, whose influence on fashion was definitive. As a gardener, he would say that his talents are few compared to those of his friend Mrs. Paul Mellon, or the interior designer Roderick Cameron, who was the previous owner of Givenchy's Clos Fiorentina. Without Mrs. Mellon the garden at Jonchet, his estate near Paris, would not be what it is today. It was her influence that gave the estate its white fences with fields and orchards on all sides, directly inspired by George Washington's estate at Mount Vernon and rather like the sheep paddocks at the hamlet of Marie-Antoinette. Mrs. Mellon also breathed a touch of folly into the vegetable garden by suggesting the planting of tuberoses among the lettuce.

Mrs. Mellon has long been recognized as an authority on all aspects of the art of living. Her knowledge of gardens, however, cannot be put down to simple good taste. She is an expert in this field, and her talent and originality are true gifts. Only a sort of sixth sense can account for her "visions," insights approaching the level of clairvoyance. "Let me give you an example," Givenchy begins. "There's a magnificent oak in the garden at Jonchet. It's several hundred years old and casts a perfectly round shadow with a lightly scalloped edge as it falls on a large lawn. As

we were walking one day, Mrs. Mellon drew my attention to this shadow. She told me to close my eyes and imagine the same shadow in blue. All I needed to do, she said, was chalk around the outline and then fill the inside with Siberian bluebells and Bismark hyacinths. I did as she suggested and the result was the closest thing to magic that I've ever seen. It was miraculous."

On another occasion they were pacing out the vegetable garden and came across an old wall that was almost entirely overgrown with moss. She told Givenchy that it was a very fine wall, but it would be even prettier if it were spotted with patches of red. Her suggestion was to line the wall with little stone dishes and plant each with strawberry seedlings that would grow straight up. Once again, the results were better than Givenchy could have hoped for: "It was absolutely extraordinary. From a distance, it looked like *petit point* tapestry and close-up it looked like a Fabergé flower. Except that *my* Fabergé gave a great deal of pleasure to the birds."

A white wooden fence recalls the one that encircles Mount Vernon, George Washington's home in Virginia. This idea was suggested by Givenchy's friend Mrs. Paul Mellon.

There are seemingly no limits to Bunny Mellon's fantasy. According to her, the whole garden ought to be replanted every year. "Which, of course, I simply can't afford to do," explains Givenchy. "Mrs. Mellon has this way of assessing the results of her experiments by telling you to change everything, which might sound defeatist but actually shows how enthusiastic and creative she is."

But the main attraction in Jonchet is the pruned box garden. The site is original but the present garden has been redesigned in a style that Givenchy considers more in keeping with the extremely uncluttered architecture of the seventeenth-century, brick-embossed château. Today a simple pattern of squares and circles replaces the old formal French garden, with its elaborate scrolls and curlicues that were meant to imitate damask. The extreme simplicity of the new garden suits the château's plain façade.

If formal gardens are a triumph of reason, then this one looks like the deliberations of a chess player who is flirting with the abstract. This garden arranges thirty-six thousand box plants in a surprisingly modern design—all the more surprising since Givenchy copied it from an original that belongs to the convent of the church of San Giorgio Maggiore in Venice. The people in charge not only allowed him to examine the plans, but trusted him enough to loan them to him. The borders are at

The cold colors of winter—gray, silver, steel-blue, and white— heighten the sober and imposing château (opposite), *while a light covering of snow enhances the formal garden* (below).

Warmth and exoticism distinguish Givenchy's second garden on Cap Ferrat in the south of France. A splendid view of the Mediterranean and the hills all the way to Italy can be enjoyed from a bedroom window (above). Orchids flower in the company of arum lilies by the edge of a pool (opposite), and everywhere geometry battles abundance. The garden was originally created by Roderick Cameron, and is considered one of the most beautiful in the world. Following pages: Carefully designed boxwood borders have a difficult time containing a profusion of Aspidistra elatior *and other perennials.*

their best in winter, when a powdering of hoarfrost draws attention to the rather tired comparison between the eighteenth century and Givenchy's love of refinement. Beneath its mantle of snow the garden has the look of a gentleman of Versailles in ceremonial clothing: a vision of white satin embroidered with crystals and frosted sequins.

LE CLOS FIORENTINA

After Bunny Mellon, Givenchy pays homage to Roderick Cameron, who he says deserves all the credit for the Clos Fiorentina. Cameron created the garden in Cap Ferrat of which Givenchy now considers himself the caretaker. "I've tried very hard to recreate the garden as it was in Cameron's day. I think I was lucky to have known him—his refinement never ceased to amaze me."

Roderick Cameron was a lavish host who treated every meal as if it were a grand reception. Outrageously handsome servants in turbans and pantaloons greeted guests as they entered the hall. An enormous Chinese earthenware gong called them to tables positioned differently for every meal. Each time they dripped with a different kind of luxury: one day there were plates by Picasso, the next exquisite Sèvres or Meissen porcelain. The house itself, furnished with the help of Syrie Maugham, the great interior designer between the wars, was a surprising jumble of 1940s mirrored furniture, Elizabethan tables, Baroque panels, and great jade dishes in which waterlilies floated. Despite this splendor, these convivial occasions were entirely without ceremony.

Cameron brought a touch of fantasy to everything he did, and it was never ridiculous. He was the author of innumerable decoration ideas that have since been taken up by others with less success. It was his idea, for instance, to whitewash the trunks of orange and mandarin trees. "It's common practice today," comments Hubert de Givenchy with a gentle shrug, since people think it keeps bugs away. "If things go on like this, pretty soon there won't be a single tree trunk left on the Côte d'Azur that isn't whitewashed." What the couturier finds all the more amusing is that the whitewashing was always purely decorative, and Cameron, who borrowed the idea from Iran, never pretended it was anything else. Where you see his particular genius at work is in the bouquets of white lilies that he planted around the tree trunks. Even those who think decoration is a minor art cannot deny the beauty in such harmony.

Above: *One of the terraces, where a fruit tree is surrounded by gravel, from which Givenchy and his guests can enjoy the view.*
Left: *In front of an ancient tower that once served as an ice house, citrus trees in Florentine pots sun themselves.*
Opposite: *Echiums, box, and other Mediterranean plants contribute a tangle of dense greenery to the Provençale ambiance.*

Hubert de Givenchy in the garden of which he is so fond. He is always here in the late spring and early summer, but also spends time at his apartment in Venice and at Jonchet. Here we can see how the garden is laid out on several terraces, making it seem much larger than it actually is.

Roderick Cameron was an Anglo-American writer and essayist who fell in love with the Cap Ferrat peninsula in the 1940s. He began by designing a garden for his mother, Lady Kenmaire, at her large Villa Fiorentina and then went on to design the more intimate garden of the Clos Fiorentina next door. Actually, anything would look intimate alongside the Neoclassical garden of the Villa Fiorentina, the noble proportions of which are positively grandiose. The adjacent and smaller Clos Fiorentina does look bigger than it is, however, thanks to Cameron's skillful use of every nook and cranny. He used the unevenness of the land to create a garden constructed of terraces separated by Chinese-style Chippendale balusters. The terraces are laid out like interconnecting rooms on different floors. The rose garden is the bedroom, a plot of tuberoses the boudoir. A courtyard filled with potted plants (fragrant with the scents of mint, sage, and basil) leads the way to the vegetable garden near the kitchen. A vine lies drying in the attic, and in the cellar, seeking shelter from the blistering sun, a line of moss has managed to creep under the clambering wisteria.

The Clos Fiorentina is a large, typically Provençal farmhouse with ocher walls and green shutters. Though many such houses exist in the south of France, few are so close to the sea. The garden flirts endlessly with the waves, as ripples of blue flicker among the branches all day long. Streams of irises, borders of lavender, and carpets of anemones pick out that same blue in the flowerbeds. There are few old houses in Cap Ferrat and none with such a magnificent view. But what's truly unique is that no one can see the house. This is something for which Givenchy congratulates himself: "We can see, but we can't be seen. The plants protect us. They screen us from all the laughing and shouting people and keep out the invading hoards that moor their boats below by the dozen every summer."

There has been an olive grove by the water for hundreds of years, like a remnant of ancient Greece. Others might well have removed it to make the most of the view, particularly in the 1950s when people raved about endless vistas. But Roderick Cameron was no more interested in big views then than Givenchy is interested in them today.

Above: *The outdoor dining area, shaded by a grape arbor, is a place where one can enjoy a vast panorama without being seen. It has all the elegance of Givenchy's lifestyle and still retains a bucolic atmosphere.*
Left: *The garden contains a gallery covered by white wisteria, a delightful place to take a fragrant and charming walk in spring.*

Anouska Hempel

A Very

Personal

Style

Above: *For the past ten years, Anouska Hempel mixed Japanese and Italian influences in the garden at her nineteenth-century home, which is surrounded by a moat and lies about sixty miles (one hundred kilometers) southwest of London.* Opposite: *Shaped in spheres, boxwood topiaries take on gigantic proportions.*

There is nothing accidental about the black swans gliding over the surface of the pond: they are typical of Anouska Hempel's inimitable look. One is immediately reminded of the bedroom draped in black that she created at Blake's Hotel in London. But then there is never anything accidental about the Hempel style, which she has managed to stamp on at least three different design disciplines.

She is one of the most glamorous and dynamic women in London. Now married to Sir Mark Weinberg, a South African financier who is chairman of Jacob Rothschild Assurance, Lady Weinberg is a renowned London hostess: people kill to be invited to her dinner parties, which include an eclectic mixture of royalty, tycoons, and celebrities who mix in her palatial town house in Holland Park. Every detail of her life is handled with the same ferocious attention to detail she gives to her highly successful hotel and fashion businesses.

Hempel's life today belies her origins on a sheep station several hundred miles west of Sydney, Australia. "My sense of aesthetics," she says, "came from rebelling against what I saw around me and creating what I wanted beauty to be." She was dying to get away from the dirt, flies, and snakes, and at age seventeen departed for London with her sister and just £10

The setting sun projects the shadow of a gracious decorative element onto the door to the walled kitchen garden.

between them. She soon married Constantine Hempel, an *Irish Times* journalist (who died in 1973 after giving her two children), had a stall in the Portobello Road antiques market, and started to pursue an acting career. The Hempels invested their savings in a rooming house in South Kensington, and that was eventually to become Blake's, one of the most elegant hotels in the world, where every room is decorated in a different way, and each bears her imprint. It was opened in 1978, and exactly ten years later she opened her own fashion house, although she had no formal training in the field.

Her couture dresses have been worn by Princess Diana, the Duchess of York, and most of the trendy ladies in London. The salon on Pond Place in Chelsea has midnight blue silk walls and swagged curtains, ebony and gilt-trimmed Regency chairs, and her clothes bear the solid structure that characterizes everything she does. "If you don't have structure, you can forget about the frills," she likes to say. Despite all this frenzied activity, Lord and Lady Weinberg set off fairly early most Friday afternoons

for their beautiful house in Wiltshire, where she wields a pair of pruning shears with the same energy and sharp eye that she uses to cut a dress. Hempel describes her garden in Wiltshire as a mixture of Zen and Italian Renaissance, and insists that there is nothing British about it. She's right: this isn't a classic English garden, but it *is* the product of English weather. Her meaning is somewhat obscure, though, considering the Queen Anne–style brick manor house and the surrounding countryside. If this isn't an English garden in the formal sense of the word, such features as a tower built in the sixteenth century by King Henry VIII are too British for the garden to remain unaffected. The Italian Renaissance style that Hempel is so proud of looks as Italian as Shakespeare's *Romeo and Juliet.* And the notorious climate certainly has its virtues: no Italian garden could ever be this divine green embellished with white roses.

The garden is especially green because of the year-round rains. Hempel is fairly philosophical about the rain, regarding it as a neces-

Above: *A sunk fence, discretely curving around the estate, naturally prolongs the view to the surrounding countryside.* Following pages: *Topiary art in all its splendor: at the foot of the stone obelisks, Hempel has assembled pots of box trimmed into large spheres and privet* (Ligustrum) *pruned into small globes at the tops of their slender trunks.*

Above: *Shrouded by the
exuberant vegetation of
climbing vines, decorative
plates grace the brick wall
that encloses the outdoor
dining area. Below them,
potted plants have pride
of place.*
Below: *A bed of fine
gravel flanked by two
rows of square pots filled
with ornamental cabbage
make an attractive setting
for this table*

sary evil. Even if the absence of sun is unbearable sometimes, she has
learned to make the most of things she cannot change: "This way, the
garden is never short of water." A humorist once said that the only way
to make the most of the English summer was to stick it in a glass frame
and hang it on the wall above the mantelpiece with a good fire burning. The often miserable summer weather is at its most dreary in July
and August. "A solid stream of cold, wet days that you think will never
end," sighs Hempel. "The weather only starts to turn fine in

September and October, and sometimes it lasts till November. Then we get some glorious days and a feast of colors that grows richer and richer with every falling leaf."

Not surprisingly, autumn is her favorite season. Among the reasons is the imposing avenue of chestnut trees that crosses the property and leads towards the manor house. As the leaves begin to turn, they blaze a trail of burnished gold through the green countryside, strewing the ground with a riot of color. The hump-backed bridge over the fairly large pond beyond makes the manor house appear to stand on an island. The brick wall at the back of the house is festooned in red garlands of Virginia creeper. This is where the garden proper begins. Hempel's fondness for pruned yew and box has given the site a geometric style of extraordinary variety and imagination, presenting an uncommon vision: fantasy at its straightest, expressed as a criss-cross pattern of squares that holds the plants in tightly packed rows. This desire for discipline and order is all

The brick path laid out in a herringbone pattern, along with borders lined in box and the alternating patterns of earth and gravel, all contribute to the geometric style of this walled kitchen garden, which is reinforced by the arches, built to be covered with vines.

There is a subtle marriage of vegetable and mineral worlds in the box topiaries and alternating areas of earth and gravel (below left), and in a gravel checkerboard surrounded by a small hedge of rosemary (below right). In the kitchen garden Hempel devised bentwood structures, which are perfect for such climbing plants as beans (opposite).

around. The orchard, the vegetable garden, and the green fields even fall into a pattern like kaleidoscopic images.

Most of the paths are graveled or paved with small bricks in a herringbone pattern. In addition to being walkways, many of them are also part of the graphic flowerbed designs: semicircular, square, gridded, zigzag, and star- or sun-shaped. Hempel has used topiary to suit her own needs, improvising jacquards, mosaics, and puzzles as evocative of Op Art as of Land Art. But this particular form of Land Art has a charmingly feminine look—more tapestry than monolith. "It must be ten years since I started this garden, and it will probably keep me busy till the day I die," says Hempel rather wistfully while lopping off an unruly branch. Her boundless energy enables her to do a thousand things at once, and all of them properly. She says she never stops, but doesn't even notice it. "That's how you live when you feel passionately about things: you don't stop for a moment. When I'm traveling, the minute I see a color combination or mixture of plants that appeals to me, I start to think what I could do with it." She learned about this integration of gardening and the art of living in Japan, where it is perhaps better understood than elsewhere. There, the economy of means applied approaches abstraction.

Hempel uses this same economy to get the most out of the simplest elements. In fact she uses relatively few plants and no rare species at all. But the way she combines the plants and the gravel, for instance, is nothing short of prodigious. The interplay between these two elements invokes a playful form of Zen. The gravel is mostly used in contrasting colors and with wide strips of black earth to form a marquetry pattern similar to the paving in certain Italian churches. Brick serves the same purpose in the aromatic garden, where red intensifies a series of glazes ranging from deepest green to blue. The vegetable garden in the shape of a star is so extraordinary that it's almost a surprise to find vegetables growing there.

Occasional splashes of lawn serve to show off arrangements of potted plants that conform to the principles of topiary. It becomes clear that Hempel, as an interior designer, took great joy in juxtaposing bushes pruned to look like balls with solid granite spheres, or obelisks formed by branches with obelisks made of stone. But she resists such accurate labels as interior designer, landscape artist, fashion designer, and gourmet, and bridles if you try to tie her in too closely with the narrow world of London fashion design. "London doesn't own me any more than Tokyo or Sydney do," she protests. "I think what I do is international."

Opposite: The garden contains a lovely Victorian hothouse, where an orange tree cohabits with gardenias, jasmine, and geraniums, whose leaves exhale a delicious perfume.

Anouska Hempel is an eclectic stylist, and always surprises friends and guests at her renowned Blake's Hotel with highly unusual touches. The same can be said of her country house, where she mixes a rose among the blackberries (above), and sends American black swans around the moat of her house (below).

Hermès

A Scarf

in the Sky

Opposite: *This small roof garden offers a bit of nature that is deeply appreciated in the heart of Paris. At 24 Rue du Faubourg St. Honoré, a gigantic lead horseman waves two Hermès silk scarves before the neighbors' roofs. In the greenery, the square form of the scarves frames the base of a bust (above) that nestles into the garden.*
Following pages: *Despite its diminutive size, the garden includes a large apple tree, a luxuriant camellia, as well as a small lawn and rosemary bushes, all enlivened by impatiens.*

The Hermès address is immortalized in a perfume called "24 Faubourg," and everyone in Paris knows it by heart—not just the number, but the image and site. Every true Parisian considers Hermès to be part of their culture, and it's easy to see why. The House of Hermès has occupied the same corner building since 1879, and it has always been an irresistible attraction to all lovers of fine things. Most of them would never guess that there is a tiny garden growing on the roof. From street level the railings are barely visible, and the only evidence of the plants is the vague outline of branches. Much more visible is the horseman that projects over the front of the building, strutting about like a giant tin soldier, half turning to the left and then to the right, waving his two silk banners (Hermès scarves both of them—and, as the horseman proves, they are very durable). If he were to fall backwards, the little garden would be his final resting place.

Only the initiated are allowed up to the terrace—the privileged few who meet with Jean-Louis Dumas Hermès in his office and discover the garden into which it extends. In 1970, when some of the manufacturing workshops were relocated to the nearby suburb of Pantin, he converted what was then attic space into his office.

Left: *Yasmina Den Mati, who conceived the garden and maintains it, has given priority to white. In the springtime, a pot under the flowering apple tree makes up a scene of the utmost purity, mixing creamy yellow tulips and white pansies with narcissus.*

Above right: *In summer, the spring bulbs and pansies are replaced by white impatiens that flower from May to the first frost, as generously in a pot as in the flower beds.*

Sometimes he's quite willing to play host and give guided tours. "The glove factory was here," he explains. "In fine weather, the girls used to spend their lunch hour sunbathing behind a little wall that was knocked down in the course of building." Referring to the head of a business in his place of work as the host reflects the unusually close relationship that exists between the House of Hermès and the Hermès family. A flood of childhood memories, many of them secondhand, only adds to the confusion. Dumas reels off details that he cannot possibly remember, including that Barbara Hutton used to climb the stairs to the workshop to personally select the hides from which she wanted her gloves made (every year, she ordered twelve dozen pairs and wore each pair only once). Passed down by word of mouth, such details are so much a part of his psyche that we can almost see him juggling enormous orders of gloves destined for an American millionairess.

There is magic in the way Dumas brings the past to life. Using an assortment of anecdotes and memories, he conjures up a world that now seems charmingly small-town and old-fashioned. He summons up Mademoiselle Marquier, one of the first salesgirls, who used to pose on this terrace for Monsieur Camille Marquier, a manager who would create an ongoing photographic record of new designs.

Next, he reveals the exact place where a length of silk commemorating the Entente Cordiale was kept hidden from the Germans during World War II. "Right here," he says, pointing to a trap-door. From his description of the banner painted with the English and French flags, one senses what he felt when Paris was liberated and the building was festooned in garlands of red, white, and blue silk. His emotion is also apparent at the sight of the little orange tree and the tulip bulbs—both gifts from former associates.

The structure of the terrace hasn't changed much over the years. The original railings and the wooden trellis now form panels with "Hermès" written in bold characters at the top. The little path still follows the railings and overhangs the garden. Jean-Louis Dumas says this makes him feel protected, as if his fragrant garden were a burrow. The fantastic numbers of birds that flock here from all sides seem to agree with him. "There are so many of them that sometimes you have to keep them quiet just to be able to work in peace," he says, but judging from the charming birdhouse that hangs from the branch of an apple tree, their presence is not unwelcome. Apart from the camellia, this is the only tree and quite

This is the window of Dumas's office, looking out on the garden. A hollyhock brings out its deep pink pompoms. Dumas is a nature lover, grows grapes in his office, and is particularly privileged to seek inspiration and energy in his lofty garden. Few people can imagine that this delightful Eden is floating above the busiest and most elegant shopping street in Paris.

Above: *Soil brought from Normandy and copious watering nourish the apple tree and enable it to bear fruit in the hot, dry Paris summers.*
Opposite: *A cupid plays hide-and-seek behind a screen of branches and leaves.*

enough to shade the lawn dotted with paving stones. Thanks to Dumas's cousin, Patrick, this apple tree has its roots in its native Normandy soil. Dumas had been thinking about converting the terrace into a garden for some time, but probably would not have done so had his cousin not built a swimming pool at his Normandy estate. The soil left over from digging the pool was more than enough to plant the Hermès garden in Paris, and now Dumas can play at being an apple farmer in Paris.

In the spring the garden is abloom with white flowers: first crocuses, pansies, and primroses, then clematis and hollyhocks. Limited space required Dumas to be fairly selective. A multicolored extravaganza would look untidy in such a small area, so that was clearly not an option. Fortunately Dumas had always favored gardens of white flowers. The resulting garden, with its lawn in the middle and box hedges and little white flowers saddle-stitched all around, is reminiscent of a *carré*, the French word not only for "square," but also for the silk scarf that, along with saddlery and luggage, has made the name Hermès so famous. The resemblance is both deliberate and, given the scale of the garden, difficult to miss. It is plainly a green and white *carré* with the soft grayish tones of aromatic plants, mainly sage and rosemary. It is also a celebration of nature by a devoted admirer and one whose environmental conscience is also apparent in the recent creation of some Hermès bags made of "Amazonia," a new rubber-based vegetable material made by indigenous people of the Amazon valley.

In this little garden Dumas can feel close to nature right in the middle of Paris. When he returns tired and jet-lagged from one of his innumerable trips abroad, this is the little piece of paradise that awaits him. The seasons change as he watches from his terrace. He marks the changing seasons on his terrace, exclaiming, "I've seen this garden under eight inches of snow!" The terrace also appears to extend further to the west due to a tiny bow window on the other side of the office that he uses as his greenhouse. When the Marquis de Lure Salus gave him two of his Château d'Yquem vines, this is where Jean-Louis Dumas planted them. Both are of noble lineage, and both now yield a yearly harvest. Well almost. Jean-Louis Dumas triumphantly reports that there were two bunches the first year, none the second year, and then a magnificent bunch last year that "was worth all the effort. As the Marquis de Lure Salus remarked, it was a sure sign that the House of Hermès puts quality before quantity."

Stephan Janson

An Iris Lover in Tangier

Above: *In the secret patios of his luxuriant garden in Tangier, Stephan Janson has not only saved such endangered species as the* Iris tingitana, *but also surrounds himself with beautiful orchids, papyrus, and aquatic plants.* Opposite: *Imposing palm trees jut above the crenellated roof of the house.*

To be the subject of a communication from the Iris Society is, for iris enthusiasts, a consecration of the highest level. Stephan Janson confirms that he was as surprised as honored. Because he lives all year in Milan, where he opened a ready-to-wear house, and only devotes himself to gardening when staying at Tebarek Allah, his villa in Tangier, he never aspired to be more than an amateur gardener. But even without any special training, Janson knew how to plant the *tingitana* bulb he found in the undergrowth. Although he didn't realize it, he was conducting a rescue mission—the species was very nearly extinct. Since being rescued, "the phoenix of the growth of this wood" has reproduced and more than a hundred specimens now grow, despite the splendor of the species. Treasured since antiquity for its dark, extremely dense, violet color, the *Iris tingitana* is today very much the star of Tebarek Allah. It is not only given pride of place within the garden, but also holds court at the entrance to the house, in pots that are taken out with great care on the first beautiful days.

It is difficult not to be bowled over by the *tingitana's* beauty, but Janson does nothing to encourage its worship. He even looks a bit embarrassed

On the patio of the Tangier house (above and opposite), pots of fuschia and cane begonias flourish in the company of a beautiful evergreen fern. Nephrolepis. The rather haphazard arrangement of plants is very much in keeping with Janson's idea of creative disorder.

by the reverence the flower inspires, and in his features appear the pride and confusion of a paterfamilias whose offspring display their gifts almost arrogantly. And though the *tingitana* attracts the most attention, it is by no means the only flower Janson has successfully planted here. In fact, transplanting is one of his favorite pastimes, and Tebarek Allah has become a refuge for local flora. The area around Tangier is an endless nature preserve, with at least twelve species of mimosa flowering in their natural state on the nearby hills (Janson has domesticated three at his house). Skunk cabbage *(Lysichiton)* and arum also grow there, and even orchids reproduce in the wild without the aid of a gardener. Saving one from the wheels of a car is among Janson's proudest accomplishments. The orchid not only survived, but blooms every year. The *Scilla peruviana* is yet another example of successful reintegration. At first it is difficult to think of it as a wildflower, but he found this astonishing raceme of mauve flowers in the countryside too.

Janson discovered Tangier by chance in the late 1980s, when he fled Marrakech, which had become too touristy for his taste. The postcolonial atmosphere then prevalent in Tangier was more in keeping with his needs, and he was immediately captivated by the atmosphere of this sleepy town. "Things are changing because of the attraction of this region for people from the Gulf," he explains. "But at the time a sort of immobility—which might have turned into a coma—reigned over the life of the city." It was easy to find villas to rent, and many were for sale. A number of them had been abandoned and waited, with their disheveled gardens, for their dormant beauty to be reawakened. The local society perpetuated the colonial combination of cosmopolitan sophistication and small-town gossip. But even if the fauna amused Janson, it was the flora that convinced him to stay.

Janson presents his garden as the result of a considerable number of experiences, mistakes even. "Here," he explains, "errors have little consequence. When you go wrong, you just start again." Having found a neat and tidy garden, albeit much smaller than those of his neighbors, he decided to turn it into a jungle in which it is difficult to find one's way. He feels certain that the former owner had tried to save water, time, or energy, since he discovered that he need only water regularly to grow the most varied species from daisies to tuberoses. Like a horror-movie monster that outgrows its creator, the garden soon took on a life of its own, and the absence of discipline is quite striking when one arrives at

Opposite: *The typically Moroccan ambiance is generated by the design of the ceramics as well as the exuberant vegetation—a climbing vine,* Pandorea jasminoides, *a white cane begonia, and, in the foreground, the ample foliage of a banana tree.*
Below: *The corner of another patio offers an intimate scene with a beautiful pot of maidenhair fern, the fronds of which are exceptionally delicate.*

Above: *Surrounding two pavilions, a completely enclosed garden contains a pool and the incredibly luxuriant vegetation of elephant ears,* Alocasia, *and a* Farfugium japonicum *with rounded leaves.*

Above: *All year-round, meals take place outside in the shade of an arbor covered with the morning glory,* Ipomoea indica, *at the foot of which blooms a profusion of petunias and African marigolds.* Opposite: *Bunches of zinnias and African marigolds enliven another dining area on a patio shaded by a thick canopy of vines.*

Tebarek Allah, particularly since the entrance is a curtain of enormous leaves that, while welcoming the visitor, bar his way. (Janson learned from a plants book that the bush's botanical name is *Monstera Deliciosa.*) This first obstacle, once conquered, leads to a path lined with dozens of potted plants: roses, fruit trees, hibiscus, and wild lavender among them. They are moved according to the season, and to follow sun and shade, which each needs in different amounts.

The path to the main house passes a pond where waterlilies, hyacinths, and papyrus—as well as goldfish and frogs—live in perfect harmony. Beyond a wisteria leaning against a pepper tree are a hundred-year-old cedar and a terrace, on which intertwined hanging plants form a cascade with gaps and loose strands; Janson compares the overall appearance to an old tapestry. This curtain of flowers produces delicious perfumes dominated by jasmine and rose. Even the outdoor dining areas are shaded by arbors—one covered with morning glory—with petunias and African marigolds below, another with bunches of zinnias and vines. At the foot of the cedar, which predates the house and is more than sixty-five feet (twenty meters) tall, is a similar confusion of geraniums, plumbago, cacti, roses, and tiny pale-green to ivory night jasmine (*Cestrum nocturnum*) flowers, whose sweet perfume mingles with warm drafts and other fragrances on a summer night.

From the high point at the top of the steps leading to the second half of the garden, one would expect an endless view of the sky above and the

sea below. But Janson decided against expansiveness here, opting instead for the lush surround of dense and disorderly vegetation that prevents a clear overview. In no other part of the garden is the jungle effect so pronounced. Highlights appear almost as discoveries—rose bushes, a Judas tree, yellow iris, a rock that looks sculpted—then recede into the jumble as the path leads through areas of green, terraces, and flowered enclosures, each of which presents different combinations of the blossoming plants seen throughout. In the North African climate, nature favors exchanges where concupiscence knows no limits. Here the most unlikely unions triumph over the ordinary combinations, and it is quite natural to see small plants dominating their larger neighbors: a rose greedily wraps around a cactus, and microscopic flowers conquer hundred-year-old trees. Elsewhere this would be madness, but here everything succumbs to a spirit of unreasonableness, thus fulfilling the wishes of the owner of the property.

If Janson sometimes does not finish his sentences it is only due to his desire to furnish the most information possible without boring the listener. This discretion is central to his character: reserved, even distracted, he was well brought-up and never gives the impression of being pushy. Though he made his career in Milan, he has little in common with the type of designer often seen dripping with portable telephones and the latest fashions in Italy's ready-to-wear capital. He stands apart,

Below: *Janson has planted geraniums at the foot of a carved stone gourd.*

Opposite: *When grown in the hot climate of Tangier, papyrus can attain impressive height, sometimes surpassing six feet (two meters).*
Right: *Nephrolepis ferns luxuriate in shaded pots next to a splendid carved stone trough.*

Below: *Janson has emphasized the function of pools as havens of coolness by placing them in shaded patios. Here numerous aquatic plants, notably papyrus and Salvinia natans, share space with a Nephrolepis fern and a Solanum wendlandii.*
Opposite: *A bougainvillea is reflected in the water of this pool, in which the round leaves of waterlilies float against a background of water hyacinth, Eichornia crassipes.*

and this independence of spirit was crucial to founding a ready-to-wear atelier for private clients in Milan. He quickly attracted members of the top ranks of society, who felt out of place in an often aggressive fashion scene. With them Janson formed a pocket of resistance to the shifting dictates of fashion.

Janson claims that chance played the greatest role in helping him achieve this position. Chance brought him in touch with Yves Saint Laurent; only by chance did he meet Diane von Furstenberg, near whom he worked for six years in New York; and chance finally led him to Milan, where he was to make his career. His trust in chance is also found in the garden, which he does not try to control. It resembles a miniature jungle—nearly a potted jungle—inhabited by a thoughtful and romantic young man.

Kenzo

*Roots in
the Bastille*

*Above: While sitting on
the terrace adjoining his
bedroom, an area
embellished by bamboo
screens, Kenzo's
contemplation of his lovely
garden transports him
back to his native Japan.
The garden (following
pages) is dominated by a
pond, and is maintained
according to Japanese
tradition by Mr. Iwaki, a
renowned Japanese
landscape designer. In the
foreground, a tsukubai,
decorated with flowers, is
ready for the traditional
tea ceremony. Around the
water are rocks, bamboo,
Japanese maples and
hostas.
Opposite: A rather
common impatiens is
endowed with a certain
exoticism by a Japanese
glazed vessel.*

The double meaning of the word "roots" is especially applicable in the case of Kenzo, who has created an authentic Japanese garden near the Bastille in Paris, thousands of miles from his birthplace in Japan. This garden expresses Japanese culture first and foremost, but it also returns Kenzo to his formative years, when he was a little boy in a small village situated in the shadow of the great Himeji castle dreaming of his future. Everything that Kenzo hoped for when he left Japan for Paris, against his parents' wishes, has come true a thousand times over.

When he left Tokyo for Paris it was like going to the ends of the earth—the boat trip took over six weeks, and there were numerous stops along the way. But dreamers are sometimes more determined and stubborn than people who have their feet firmly on the ground, and Kenzo dared to believe in things that would not have occurred to more realistic people. He overcame his family's resistance and made the long trip.

Paris in the 1960s still had that air of untroubled relaxation that Kenzo found so appealing, but it was also an exhilarating place to live. Today his head office on the Place des Victoires is not far from the Galerie Vivienne, where he opened his first boutique. But the road he has traveled between the two is almost as extraordinary as the distance from Paris to Tokyo. The most striking feature of the boutique in the Galerie

The view from Kenzo's room focuses attention on the artistically twisted branches of the Japanese maples and the play of their leaves over the rocks and water below. A collection of lovely blue Japanese porcelain completes the scene.

Vivienne, which he set up with some friends in less than a month, is how fresh it is. He called it "Jungle Jap" as a joke, and that humor set the tone for both the interior design and the clothes. But Kenzo has brightened this, and many other jungles, with flowers during the course of his career—it's a language he understands.

There is nothing rustic about the Bastille area where Kenzo chose to live. Even when Paris still had gardens and farmers' markets, this area was most notorious for its misguided youth. In the French mind, the Bastille has stood for the end of the *ancien régime:* a hotbed of revolution famous for its *sans-culotte,* for its heroes, and for its hooligans and call girls. The Bastille area started to change in the 1980s, but has remained predominantly working-class and easygoing. Today it is home to a great many young people, as well as artists, who need large floor areas that can be converted into studios at reasonable prices. Most of the old craftsmen have disappeared, but the new local color has revived the folklore of the Bastille without spoiling it altogether. It's not poor anymore, but it's just as Bohemian as ever.

Further evidence of Kenzo's single-mindedness is found in how completely out of place his serene Japanese garden is in this neighborhood. His strong will had brought him to Paris and made possible his many accomplishments, and it would also often be the only force keeping him from giving up on the garden altogether. But in many cases, from the positioning of a plant to the discovery of the actual building, he was bolstered by the belief that everything would be made perfect in good time. He is a man who knows what he wants, and needs only to be patient—or driven—enough to get it. He chose a disused furniture factory because it fulfilled his two requirements: warehouses and sufficient space for a Japanese garden. "When I found it," Kenzo recalls, "there was an open-air space where I knew the garden had to go. There was simply nowhere else for it." This is apparent in the finished garden, too: while there is nothing natural about the entire garden, everything is just where it should be (except that it's one flight up from street level). The perfect balance and harmony obscure the immense amount of work that was involved. "What makes a Japanese garden look so simple," says Kenzo, "are all the things that you don't see." In a scene from *2001: A Space Odyssey*, one of the astronauts pushes open a door and finds himself face-to-face with an ornate Louis XV bedroom right in the heart of infinity. The effect is similar in Kenzo's garden: visitors feel that they have forced their way into a place of unexpected beauty, intruded on the designer's privacy. The sense of disorientation has the unreality of a fairytale.

There was a time when Kenzo thought he would limit himself to bamboo, a cherry tree, and a maple tree. The result was pretty, but not enough. A real Japanese garden has to have a river, waterfalls, fish, and other elements. Even though the garden is relatively modest in size, he was obliged to build on a large scale and to send for a landscape artist from Japan to ensure authenticity.

"The landscape artist was Mr. Iwaki, and he's very famous in Japan," says Kenzo, with some pride. "The first time he came to Paris was to see the model. He returned later when the work started, which took forever because we had enormous problems with the waterproofing—that's what happens when you try to hang a river from the first floor. It also took us a long time to find the right position for the stones I ordered from Japan. The carp seem extremely happy here now," he says, displaying his legendary smile.

Below: *Such beautiful bark could only belong to a Japanese cherry tree, the Prunus serrulata.* Bottom: *Perfection and delicacy mark the flower of the arum lily, which prospers on the humid shores of the pool.*

That smile was put to the test on many occasions while the work was in progress. Before the house was finished, Mr. Iwaki planted a Japanese cherry tree and a fir tree. They didn't survive due to the construction, lack of soil, and climate. Kenzo nearly went mad. "I lost two fir trees, both of them magnificent, and in the end I lost the cherry tree, too, because of the cold." Then the bamboo froze in the Parisian winter, which was a real catastrophe. But his luck changed when he met a nurseryman at the Bienniale des Antiquaires in Paris. His name was Crouzet, and he happened to cultivate a tougher breed of bamboo on his farm in Anduze. One of Kenzo's greatest annual luxuries is to bring over a gardener from Japan who prunes and cares for the plants in the time-honored fashion. "Japanese gardens have to be looked after in a certain way, and it's something you have to learn. It looks simple, but there are a thousand different details to think about."

Today Kenzo has every right to be proud of the nearly authentic result. "European maple," he explains, "doesn't look like Japanese maple. It's much finer over there, much more delicate, much lacier." Regardless of its origin, every autumn this maple turns a vivid red and pours its color into the clear waters, and Kenzo's pleasure knows no bounds. The city falls silent then, and all he hears is the wind whispering through the bamboo. He can retreat within himself, close his eyes, and watch the red of the maple leaves merging and dancing with the red of the goldfish.

Three scenes worthy of a Japanese print: the admirable shadows cast by the diaphanous stalks of a bamboo (above); the graceful koi swimming in the pool (left); and the exquisite and delicate flowering of an orchid. Oncidium (opposite).

Michel Klein

Outdoor

Interiors

Above: *"Relaxed" is the word that best describes both the personality of Michel Klein and the style of the garden he created, not without trouble, near Saint-Rémy-de-Provence. Opposite: An aralia, Fatsia japonica, unfolds its admirably structured and ample foliage.*

The Côte d'Azur, the Alpilles and the Lubéron are a trilogy of holiday resorts, one flowing into the other. When too many tourists made the Côte d'Azur undesirable, then people retreated to the hinterland, what the French call *"l'arrière-pays."* The area has become particularly accessible thanks to the TGV superspeed trains from Paris to Aix-en-Provence, and numerous flights to Marseilles and Avignon. The rocky landscape, which inspired Cézanne and van Gogh, lavender-filled fields, three-star restaurants, Roman ruins, and world-renowned music festivals are only some of the delights that have created a frenzy of property purchases and building. The *mas de Provence*—newly built or restored local farmhouses—are now holiday headquarters for people from all over the world, and from April to October their social life can be absolutely frenetic. Visitors from England, America, and Germany are rarely obliged to utter a word in French. Much of the day is spent under a clear blue sky around a swimming pool, which is far preferable to spending hours in a traffic jam to arrive at the overcrowded beaches of the Mediterranean. And pools cry out for proper landscaping, well-trimmed hedges, bushes, potted plants, and flower beds—everything to

Preceding pages: *In front of the ancient sheep barn that has become his home, Klein has furnished the garden with, among other things, numerous pots and decorative supports for roses.*
Above: *Klein is a master at finding original, even antique furniture for his garden, living as comfortably outdoors as he would in his house. He has scoured the local dealers, particularly those on the Isle-sur-Sorgue, for such original pieces as this wrought-iron day bed, which is perfect for an afternoon nap. Complete with side table, potted plants, and a chair, his guests might well mistake this area of the garden for their bedroom.*

inspire the gardeners who have temporarily left the big city to find their Eden. Today the *arrière-pays* is home to many of the rich and famous of France: such celebrities as Pierre Bergé, Jacques Grange, Inès de la Fressange, and Caroline of Monaco. But few people realize what a peaceful, unfashionable existence these celebrities have chosen to lead there. It is precisely this quiet, unpretentious relaxation that Michel Klein, formerly the principal designer for Guy Laroche, is looking for when he hides away in Eygalières, a little village near Saint-Rémy in Provence. Klein has lived in the Latin Quarter of Saint-Germain-des-Prés in Paris since childhood, and he still values friendship over social obligations. If his friendship with Princess Caroline is public knowledge, he certainly has not advertised it. When he uses the phrase "Caroline of Monaco," it is only to refer to his roses.

One of the reasons Klein bought the house is the pair of magnificent plane trees that stand outside it. He liked them so much that he insisted that both be included in the sales contract. At the time, one of the trees

grew very close to the garden, but not close enough to be a part of it. As far as he was concerned, these trees and the house were of a piece. The house was originally a shepherd's cottage, dating back to perhaps the sixteenth or seventeenth century. It bore the marks of time, and the garden was a wreck—"a wasteland," as Klein says. That seems hard to believe today, especially on the terrace, which is as full of stuff as a Victorian sitting room. This is where breakfast is eaten, the table surrounded by an assortment of potted plants growing among the chaises longues and occasional tables. There are cloves, hydrangeas, agapanthus, a plumbago, all sorts of cacti, and a powdery sage basking in the sun. A wisteria climbs up the front of the house, pausing to intertwine with the creepers of a morning glory, whose trumpets challenge the blue of the shutters. Klein's garden is likely the most "couture" of all the designers' gardens. It is decidedly rag-trade in its plethora of bed throws, shawls, cushions, pieces of striped fabric, oddments of every description, and even carpets outdoors. Carpets, in Klein's opinion, are for use inside and out. But he brings not only carpets outside—he also brings out furniture, including tables, chairs, and even daybeds, one of the specialities of his garden. The warm climate in the south of France sanctions this process of seasonal migration. One gets the impression that for Klein a branch is primarily a place to hang a chandelier. "You're right," he says. "I'm not crazy about normal garden furniture—that predictable teak table with two armchairs and six straight chairs. You wouldn't dare put anything as bourgeois as that in your dining room these days. So why does garden

The beauty of combinations of potted plants holds no secrets for Michel Klein. Santolina, box, and datura stand against the background of a morning glory (top left), an agreeable assortment of cactus are found on a garden table (top right), and cordyline, box, agapanthus, and datura flourish in their pots (above).

furniture have to be so desperately unoriginal?" From the way his garden looks today, antique shops have plainly had as much influence as garden centers. Gardening does not mean the same to Klein as it does to most people, so he has had to design garden furniture and accessories of his own. It began when he found the perfect pots for his terrace in the flea market nearby on the Isle-sur-la-Sorgue. He took them to a local potter, who made copies. Next came furniture, fabric, cushions, and curtains. Today he even has sheets made.

Klein came to gardening relatively late in life, and since he acquired a wasteland he had to learn as he went along. Nothing daunted him, and he dreamed of a completely white garden. So did a great many others at the time, and magazines encouraged them. It took six years of work to make his dream come true, and though he maintained his enthusiasm throughout, he also had a rude awakening. In practice, white gardens are rarely as white as they are in one's dreams. The seed packet may be labeled "white flowers," but the color is often a surprise when they bloom. Klein remains mystified to this day: "When they came up, there would always be some pink, yellow, or blue ones in with the white ones, so the garden was never completely white." Not to mention what most people call weeds, often so pretty that he didn't have the heart to pull them out. His dream of a white garden was short-lived.

Top: *A pot from Aubagne is personalized with Klein's name.*
Left: *The draped chair contributes as much to the decor as the luxuriant potted hydrangea.*

Klein bought his country house at a time when there was a growing interest in gardening. He insists that this was a coincidence although, as he points out, Loulou de la Falaise acquired her garden at about this time. "It was like the end of an era. Suddenly we were all talking seeds, cuttings, and bulbs," he recalls, desperately trying to understand how former night clubbers could suddenly become consumed by a passion for gardening. "We were like new converts, busily exchanging tips on how to plant successful flower beds or protect the seedlings." But Loulou had a rudimentary knowledge of gardening thanks to her grandmother, who was an expert. Klein knew nothing, and it's something he still regrets. All the willpower in the world is no substitute for knowing the fundamentals when it comes to handling a gardening crisis. In times of trouble Klein says the only thing he knows how to do is pull up weeds. Some of the lessons he learned from nature have proved what he learned in the field of fashion, and the painful breakup with Guy Laroche increased his appetite for the simple things in life. The pleasure he feels

Garden chairs and tables make up both physical and aesthetic support for potted plants. To be noted is the young planted cypress, which forms a background for potted cypress, all symmetrically flanked by potted agaves.

Above: *The wind waves the supple branches of the weeping willow and enhances the effect of lavender in full flower, but it has no effect on the more robust branches of the imposing white-flowered oleander in the glazed pot.*
Opposite: *In this wilder part of the garden, a bench invites respite by a tall violet wallflower (Erysimum) and the large white spikes of a yucca.*

each year when his roses bloom again is rather like some of his styles: "Because I often included the Chinese jacket in my collections, people were always accusing me of doing the same thing. But I think that was clairvoyant, given what happened to fashion. I think my taste for the stripped-down look was clairvoyant, too." Klein has risen like a phoenix from the ashes. He is now full of ideas, raring to go, and looking for a big enough place in Paris to house them all. He even wants to open the shop to other designers creating an entirely unpredictable atmosphere, with the same easy charm as his garden in Provence.

Christian Louboutin

Flights

of Fancy

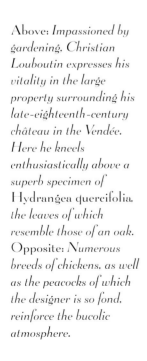

Above: *Impassioned by gardening, Christian Louboutin expresses his vitality in the large property surrounding his late-eighteenth-century château in the Vendée. Here he kneels enthusiastically above a superb specimen of* Hydrangea quercifolia, *the leaves of which resemble those of an oak. Opposite: Numerous breeds of chickens, as well as the peacocks of which the designer is so fond, reinforce the bucolic atmosphere.*

Christian Louboutin takes an excellent quince jam from a kitchen cupboard lined with jars. "I made it myself," he claims without a moment's hesitation, triggering a fit of laughter that sets the table rocking. The house is bursting at the seams with friends who have come to stay for the weekend, and Christian, who was last to get up this morning, is in for a barrage of sarcasm. As some of his friends are quick to point out, he has a peculiar ability to live on the frontiers of reality. He's been playing the "I-made-it-myself" game for two days now, and it's a game he plays better than anyone. His lively, colorful imagination makes anything he says sound believable, and it's nearly impossible to know whether he's telling the truth or lying.

If the end does indeed justify the means, however, then the magical Champgillon is well worth a few fairytales. Champgillon is actually the name of a tiny village in the Vendée, but for Louboutin it's the name of the property in which he regularly takes refuge. The estate boasts an orchard, vegetable garden, rose garden, and labyrinth. From the kitchen window a peacock can be seen strutting its stuff on the edge of a well, while all around hens rustle their feathers.

In short, there is madness in the air. This should come as no surprise, for Louboutin is never short of invention. His garden has the same aura of fantasy as his shoe collections, teeming with such crazy and occasionally outrageous ideas as his unforgettable dress shoes with red soles. What's really surprising, like everything else that seems obvious in retrospect, is that no one thought of it before him.

When Louboutin came to Champgillon he found an estate marked out by hundred-year-old trees and, at first, left it alone. But once he had become acquainted with the cedar, persimmon, ginkgo, and orange trees, he started dreaming and building castles in the air. The labyrinth created out of pruned laurel bushes was his idea, as were the crenellated wall around the vegetable garden and the field planted with annuals (amaranths, cosmos, centaurea, lavender) in decreasing shades of mauve and blue. He also unearthed the rusted greenhouse, had it restored, and positioned it where it stands today, like a corner seat between two of the château's turrets.

Above: The wildflower meadow, which Louboutin partly replanted, includes a field of such large flowering annuals as cosmos.
Opposite: Two enticing hollyhocks exhibit their red and dark-pink pompoms in front of an elegant archway.
Following pages: René Puibert, Louboutin's faithful and hardworking gardener, tends a fabulous fruit and vegetable garden.

In addition to an astonishing number of lettuces (eighteen varieties), the kitchen garden contains tempting tomatoes (below), numerous cucurbits, notably zucchini (below right), melons, and some unusual squash and pumpkins. The gardener's line is always ready to trace perfectly aligned furrows (bottom right).

Louboutin also takes pride in the eighteen varieties of lettuce that grow in the vegetable garden along with such delights as squash, rutabaga, Giraumon marrows, and winter cherries. Even the horrible disease that is currently laying waste to so many box trees proved a source of inspiration. When it started to attack the roses, he decided to maintain the original layout of the box borders, but to raise them up more than three feet above the ground, on a metal frame now dripping with clusters of green and mauve wisteria that crown the roses with their abundant locks. He will use any pretext for another inspired extravaganza. His

*Left: The magnificent entry to the estate is thickly planted with trees, some of them a hundred years old, and some, such as the Japanese persimmon and the Osage orange, very rare.
Below: Coexisting with these specimens are a number of peacocks and chickens.*

Previous page: Louboutin salvaged this ancient greenhouse and had it moved between two towers of the château.

creative genius also appears in a path lined with a mixture of giant plants and tiny flowers, creating an effect similar to those medieval tapestries in which rabbits and forget-me-nots are woven into an impressive green background.

Seeing Louboutin at work confirms that there is some truth to the rumor that he says more than he does. He buzzes around endlessly but actually achieves surprisingly little. Running from person to person, he's busy here, busy there, rushes to his bedroom to get something only to return without it, visits the people preparing lunch, then tears from the kitchen to answer the telephone, yelling as he replaces the receiver that he must fax the embroidery designs for some wedding shoes to a girlfriend who's getting married. He may lack focus, but he certainly does not lack energy. The whole house vibrates with infectious good humor and enthusiasm. No one gets more out of his friends than Christian Louboutin.

Gardening is second only to shoes in his affections. He grew interested in shoes as he was emerging from adolescence. He had already begun developing an innate talent for communication that enabled him to talk about anything and everything with an enthusiasm that verged on gushing. He also discovered that the arch of a foot, stiletto heels, and uppers held no secrets for him, and his precocious talents soon persuaded Roger Vivier to take him on as his assistant. With no great enthusiasm, he went off to school, where he discovered the aversion to technical problems

that dreamers often feel when studying. Time passed and he focused his talents on shoes. Then one day, he started to talk about gardens. That was the first sign. Most of the people around him thought it would pass, but there was real passion in his voice when he spoke.

A way with words does not make one a good gardener, but it can help a good gardener express his beliefs and share his knowledge, which is just what Louboutin has done in his authoritative articles in French *Vogue* and *House and Garden*, for which he is a correspondent. Although gardening is clearly more than just a pastime for Louboutin, his seriousness has not transformed him into a scholar, and he refuses to recognize academic or formal constraints. Just as he refuses to be bogged down by technical problems in a new shoe design, so gardens are especially interesting because they provide him with an alternative outlet for his imagination and a source of amusement—the result is that the two great loves of Christian Louboutin's life are perfectly balanced.

The view from this shaded bench extends over the surrounding meadows to beyond a thick curtain of deciduous trees and evergreens carefully trimmed into a cone.

Oscar de la Renta

An Endless

Vista

Under the guidance of the famous English landscape artist, Russell Page, Oscar de la Renta structured his immense garden in Connecticut by adding walls and hedges to split it into several "rooms." Today, his wife Annette (seen with him, above) is the garden's main instigator, but she certainly doesn't hinder her husband's horticultural passion. Opposite: A handsome nineteenth-century bronze is framed in vegetation cut to measure.

"With a landscape like that, you just enjoy the view": this is what Russell Page told Oscar de la Renta to discourage him from terracing his newly acquired estate in Connecticut. Page, the author of a treatise on English gardens that is followed by landscape artists the world over, felt that the place was quite unsuited to a garden. Today de la Renta remembers how disappointed he was when he heard this twenty-eight years ago, and how sarcastic Page could be. All the more sarcastic since he didn't seem to do it on purpose. He merely surveyed nature with that air of superiority that specialists assume when surrounded by amateurs.

But Page had another judgment to pass along. In the weeks before the master's visit, de la Renta had done a lot of work using a manual that local aspiring gardeners regarded as a bible. The book was put out by a renowned nearby nursery, and de la Renta followed the instructions to the letter. He wasn't at all sure what Page would think of it, but he couldn't wait to show him.

Page greeted de la Renta's handiwork with disbelief and a degree of horror, like a professional golfer who finds himself playing on a miniature course. "What on earth is that supposed to be?" he shouted. De la Renta, who had been so proud of his work, pretended he had no idea,

blaming everything on the previous owners. But this piece of land had plainly been ploughed and fertilized recently. Landscape artists tend to notice details like that, particularly those with the knowledge and experience of Russell Page.

Today de la Renta admits that it may have been a mistake to invite Page. "But since I'd only just met him—at the time he was doing a garden for the Frick Collection in New York—it seemed only natural to ask him to come to Litchfield Hills, which I'd only just bought. I wouldn't dream of doing such a thing today." At that time de la Renta was the darling of New York society and the head of his enormously successful fashion house. Man-of-the-moment Henry Kissinger was a friend and admirer, and later his country neighbor, and there wasn't an event in New York to which de la Renta wasn't invited. Presumably that's how he came to meet the great British landscape artist.

The incredible view to which Page had referred was unlikely to change. Oscar de la Renta owns nearly five hundred acres of land deep in the heart of Connecticut, abutting a nature preserve so vast that it seems endless. Meadows and forests undulate through the hilly landscape as far as the eye can see and everything is on a very grand scale.

The imposing red-cedar home is now painted white, and its exterior is decorated with ornate garden furniture (left and above). Dominated by agapanthus in flower, an evergreen hedge separates the terrace from a lower level (opposite).

Although the exceptional vista remains unchanged, the garden that has sprung up around the house is nothing short of miraculous. De la Renta's first lesson in gardening was a slap in the face, but it paid off. He mistakenly overlooked the fact that a garden always needs a wall; a wilderness, however beautiful, won't do. Russell Page's *idée fixe* was walls: there had to be walls. With infinite patience, de la Renta set about doing as he'd been told. He built fences, planted hedges and rows of trees one behind the other, he closed off perspectives, and did everything possible to flesh out the box borders. There were cases of rejection, of course. The rose garden froze several years running because the winters were particularly harsh but today his garden is one of the finest in the region, living proof that an English garden can be recreated in an apparently hostile environment.

De la Renta has used other landscape artists since Russell Page, including François Gaufiney, Caroline Burgess, and the horticulturist Powers Taylor. But his wife Annette has undoubtedly had the greatest influence on their garden. He jokes that they disagree on so many things that they have to garden separately to avoid an argument. "Being a Latin by nature I can't resist bright colors," he explains. "My wife, on the other hand, likes her gardens green and is always curbing my enthusiasms." To judge from the pleasure it gives him to talk about his wife, their differences cannot be very important. He refers to her constantly in matters of taste and bows to her greater experience and knowledge when it comes to gardening, as is evident from the palette of green punctuated by bouquets of white. Clearly Annette always has the last word, and the rare touches of color—here a border of sweet Williams, there a group of sunflowers—are masterful, accentuating a predominantly green canvas that ranges from acid green to silver-gray.

The house today is surrounded by a chain of greenery—the green of the generously sized vegetable garden and the pale green of the swimming pool—enhancing the air of quiet luxury. One can easily imagine how the house once looked, and just how far the present owners have come: a rustic, red-cedar farm has been transformed into an elegant country cottage. De la Renta has built extensions and painted the facade white. A colonnade now surrounds the front door, and elegant pediments crown the sash windows. What we see today is a house with a strongly Neoclassical look, reminiscent of Thomas Jefferson's Monticello, which remains the most successful expression of this style.

Below: *Decorative geese pose for eternity before a rocky outcrop.*
Opposite: *From the carpet of blue agapanthus, the view plunges to infinity over the great wooded hills of a wildlife sanctuary.*

De la Renta's original intention was to spend weekends at the house. But now Litchfields Hills is his main home, a much-needed place to drop anchor en route to New York, Paris, and Santo Domingo. New York requires no explanation. In Paris he has directed the haute couture of the House of Balmain since 1993. Santo Domingo is where he was born, and where he owns another very fine property.

De la Renta has spent his life traveling, and although his career may look like a straight road to the top, there were some ups and downs in the early days. The white beaches of Santo Domingo, heavenly though they may be, are no place for the ambitious. Realizing this, de la Renta's Spanish parents sent their son to law school in Madrid. Except that he never did study law: Balenciaga still had a fashion house in Madrid at the time, and de la Renta joined him as an apprentice. From there he went to Paris and the House of Lanvin, this time as an apprentice to Antonio del Castillo from 1961 to 1963, after which he became the ready-to-wear and haute couture designer for America's

Following page, left:
A Veronica longifolia shows off its long slender spikes, curiously and elegantly curved over at their ends.
Following page, right:
A bucolic arrangement shows the tall yellow spikes of mullein (Verbascum) mixed in with two ornamental garlic plants—Allium aflatunense with pink umbels and Allium spaerocephalon with smaller red pompoms.

Preceding pages: *The spirit of the English garden is found throughout the property, notably in this geometric green "room", harmoniously fashioned from box. In the foreground on the left, the gracious umbels of the ornamental garlic, Nectaroscordum siculum bulgaricum, meet with the velvety pink stalks of lamb's ears, Stachys byzantina.*

Opposite: *Page's plan is thoroughly respected in another area, the focal point of which is a statue nestled in a hedged alcove and framed by large trees.* Above: *The statue overlooks a low wall with steps leading to an arrangement of hedges.*

beauty queen, Elizabeth Arden. In 1965, he became a partner and the main designer at Jane Derby Inc. in New York, and two years later met Françoise de Langlade, who had succeeded Edmonde Charles Roux as editor-in-chief at French *Vogue*. Charles Roux had won France's greatest literary plum, the Prix Goncourt, and Françoise was one of the most glamorous women in France, a fixture of Paris society with a dazzling personality, powerful friends, and impeccable taste in all the arts of living—clothes, houses, decoration, food, and wine. They married, and Françoise left her job to join de la Renta in New York as French wits quipped that Edmonde had won the Goncourt while Françoise got the Oscar. The Litchfield house was bought when they were married and—while a far more modest establishment than it is today—became an exquisitely refined country retreat filled with friends. The whole world adored the happy couple, who lived life to the fullest and feared nothing. But then, Françoise discovered she had cancer, and died in 1983. Some wounds will never heal, but de la Renta carried on in his work. Soon afterwards, the enormously successful launch of a new range of perfumes crowned an already flourishing career. For thousands of women all over the world, the name Oscar de la Renta had new meaning. Litchfield Hills is about a two-hour drive from New York, and de la Renta goes there whenever he can. Sometimes he starts gardening as soon as he steps out of the car, not even bothering to change his clothes. "I couldn't tell you how many times I've realized I'm still wearing my

suit," he admits, squatting down in front of a flower bed to straighten out a stake or pull up some weeds. "There's so much to do in a garden that once you start you can't stop." For de la Renta, gardening is an immediate communion with nature that gives him a certain sort of wisdom. His reaction is immediate when he is asked what effect his love of gardening has on his fashion design. He believes that when gardening one tends to think about practical or abstract things rather than the frivolous. "When you garden," he explains, "you think as much about the weather as the passing of time. But you rarely think about fashion. When you plant a tree, for instance, you are always reminded that it will still be growing when you're no longer around to see it. You can't help but marvel at the fragility of a flower or the solidity of a tree. You can't help but think about all this beauty that surrounds us." And with a slightly forced smile, as if trying to excuse his flight of lyricism, he gestures out towards the horizon.

Below: *The sober box borders control dense waves of vegetation comprised of highly colored and perfumed honeysuckle and flowering perennials.*

Opposite: *This statue is set off to great advantage by a backdrop of Arizona cypress and achillea and nepeta for the border.*

Yves Saint Laurent

The Garden of Allah

The garden of Yves Saint
Laurent's Villa Oasis in
Marrakech was originally
created by the painter
Jacques Majorelle. It is
hardly surprising, therefore,
that audacious colors
abound here: the ocher used
in the facade complements
the dark red of a
bougainvillea (above), and
contrasts nicely with the
yellow-bordered green of a
voluminous Agave sisalana
(opposite).
Following pages: With
their scaly trunks, the palm
trees stand guard from one
end of the path to the other,
echoed by large cactus and
geraniums in pots. In the
foreground, a bougainvillea
forms a red curtain.

The perfectly straight avenues of the flat Guéliz area in Marrakech
appear dull in comparison to the tormented backstreets of the Medina.
There are few tourists in this urban quarter, built during the French
Protectorate, and it is surprising that so residential a neighborhood
exists so close to the souks. Except for the orange and lemon peddlers
whose carts line the sidewalk, there is little of interest outside. Most of
the houses hide behind mud walls and all that can be seen is the occasional shadow of a coconut palm or cypress tree. This is also the case
with the villa owned by Yves Saint Laurent and Pierre Bergé: one can
only guess at what is under the glazed tiles of the pyramid-shaped roof
that appears to float among the leafy treetops. This is Villa Oasis, pre-
viously Villa Bou Saf-Saf, famous for the tropical garden planted there
by the painter Jacques Majorelle.

Most of the grand houses of the Guéliz area were built in the Spanish-
Moorish style by colonial architects who tried, with mixed results, to
emulate the Alhambra. Jacques Majorelle used his talents as a colorist
to transform his villa into the purest expression of that style. Saint
Laurent has honored Majorelle's plan in every detail. At the end of a
path lined with pink oleanders a brick doorway frames a green door.

Above left: *A terrace of the house overlooks a riot of vegetation: geraniums, palm trees, bamboo, and a dark pink bougainvillea.* Above right: *Mexican cactus are perfectly acclimated to Marrakech, thus these giant Stenocereus marginatus, at the foot of which nestle white crinums, Crinum x powelli 'Album.'*

Beyond lies a strident gamut of color that symbolizes the North African climate. It lashes out again further on, down cement alleys steeped in red where riotous inflections of violet and pink—bougainvillea, geraniums, datura, and hibiscus—hurl themselves against the ultramarine blue of the walls. The garden was originally designed in the classic Islamic style, the ancient spirit of which can be seen in the network of canals that run parallel to the paths. Without this constant irrigation, there would be no plants and no pools, no lilies and lotus flowers floating on the water, no papyrus, and no bamboo.

The best-known member of the Majorelle family was Jacques's father, Louis. He was one of the pioneers of a decorative style that marked the first serious challenge to the prevailingly bourgeois taste of the early twentieth century. Majorelle furniture is all scrolls and curlicues and plainly has much in common with the work of Loïe Fuller, Alfons Mucha, and Lalique jewelry. By today's standards it seems unnecessarily fussy, but for his contemporaries, Majorelle was the very essence of what would become Art Nouveau. For more than a century people had been rehashing old ideas, but Louis Majorelle did something that was certainly new. Others would imitate and develop his style, but his son Jacques would take after his spirit of innovation.

First Jacques followed his father into the decorative arts, but when he took ill a family friend suggested a restorative trip to Morocco. He never returned. In 1923 he built the villa, extending the grounds in 1932, when he bought nearly three adjacent acres on which he grew plants from around the world. Today Majorelle is remembered primarily for his garden, which has been beautifully restored by its new owners Yves Saint Laurent and Pierre Bergé. Their involvement brought the interest of fashion writers, most of whom had never heard of Majorelle before. In fact, Yves Saint Laurent is an aesthetic descendant of Jacques Majorelle. Who could better understand Majorelle's subtle balance of art and nature in his garden than a designer raised in North Africa? Saint Laurent even dreams of emulating Majorelle by leaving behind the pressures of work and coming to Marrakech for good.

When Saint Laurent took over from Dior at the age of twenty-one, he started out where most designers dream of ending up: at the top. A few years later he rose still higher when he opened his own fashion house. In the 1960s, Yves Saint Laurent collided head-on with the times, and the force of that explosion rocked the fashion world. In fewer than ten years, he paved the way for a look that would dominate female fashion throughout the rest of the century. He was the creator of the masculine-feminine look, an instant classic most perfectly represented in the "smoking," or dinner jacket. Saint Laurent was at the cutting edge of his profession. Like Louis Majorelle, his innovations may seem a bit tame by today's standards, but at the time they were as revolutionary as hurling paving stones at riot police in the streets of Paris. Saint Laurent fashion gave the students what they wanted before they even rioted for it in May of 1968. They clamored for sexual freedom, he gave them bare breasts. They wanted feminism, he gave them pant suits. They wanted escape, he gave them the safari jacket. In 1969, he did it once more, proving himself a designer ahead of his time through his 1940s-inspired retro collection, delivering nostalgia before it became a mania.

Saint Laurent's rapid rise had its price. He has never attempted to hide his weaknesses or doubts, his nervous breakdowns and fits of anguish. But anguish and elation are merely two sides of the same coin. Anguish

Saint Laurent's Marrakech garden contains a seemingly infinite number of exotic plants, starting with the cactus, Stenocereus marginatus *(below) and the* Agave americana *(bottom).*

Above: *Against a background of oleander and bamboo, cactus in pots painted turquoise or pastel blue surround a fountain.*
Opposite, top: *The perfect symmetry of the pool and potted plants is given a vague nuance of disorder by its skillfully maintained, opulent vegetation—a banana tree, bougainvillea, and oleander.*
Opposite, bottom: *The bright red flowers of a kalanchoe makes a vivid contrast to the milky blue of the pottery.*

often helps artists to think creatively in moments of great inspiration. Before he devoted himself exclusively to haute couture, he was expected to have these moments of great inspiration four times a year at a precise date. He was under constant pressure, which took its toll. Marrakech was like a soothing balm. It relieved the stress and calmed his nerves. Betty Catroux, his former muse and still his closest friend, says, "Paris seems to mirror all the anguish, Marrakech is a place of happiness." But it would be a mistake to think of the Villa Oasis as an escape from fashion. On the contrary, visitors to the Majorelle garden find themselves immersed in a bath of color reminiscent of some of the most flamboyant periods in the history of the master of the house.

The first thing Saint Laurent did when he moved in was to restore the sun-bleached colors to their original intensity. He also added several mad touches of his own. The ocher walls, for example, and the almost turquoise green of the balconies and pergola that seems to liquefy and blend with the sun against the glazed tiles. There is the ultramarine

color known as "Majorelle blue" on the walls of Majorelle's summer house, the kind of blue that evokes Matisse. Majorelle built this house right in the center of the garden as a place where he could shut himself away and paint.

If the garden is as flashy as a scene out of the *Arabian Nights*, there is nothing mawkish about its eastern origins. It is an Art-Deco hybrid that, on the contrary, expresses itself through strong colors and simple volumes. A tour today ends with a visit to Majorelle's workshop, now a museum of Islamic art containing a wealth of Moroccan porcelain, jewelry, carpets, embroidery, and pottery.

Saint Laurent and Pierre Bergé were renting the villa when they heard of a potentially disastrous property deal. The house and garden were to be sold separately, and Majorelle's collection of plants would be at the mercy of property developers. Saint Laurent and Bergé were horrified, and offered to buy the house and garden together. They also took steps to have the estate classified as a national monument. Next, believing that

charity starts at home, they launched a crusade to save the garden, knowing that this was in everyone's best interest, especially their own. Others agreed, including the King of Morocco, who banned all forms of construction on the site, and the garden was officially saved. The land lost its speculative value, and the owner wanted only to get rid of it. The sale was a mere formality. Saint Laurent and Bergé were now the owners, but in accordance with the wishes of Jacques Majorelle they kept the garden open to the public, and even planned their own program of work around the visiting hours.

Thirty years ago Bergé and Saint Laurent discovered an overgrown paradise. Since Majorelle's death, the vegetation had grown so dense in places that it virtually shut out all light, and what little light did filter through revealed an accumulation of dust that gave an idea of the Herculean task in store. The jungle-like garden was in a state of vegetative abandon that was not without charm, but that threatened to compromise its harmony if allowed to persist. Banana trees, palms, ficus, and yuccas gobbled up more than their fair share of land. The cacti in particular, left to their own devices for so long, had in some cases grown positively arborescent.

Today, the Majorelle garden is serene and orderly once again. It welcomes two hundred thousand visitors a year, and no tour of Marrakech is complete without it. Most of the species that grow here form part of the North African flora and they flourish in the dry, sunny climate. They are at home where they are, rooted in a rainbow.

Valentino

The Baroque in Nature·

For Valentino Garavani, being a big fish in a small pond was never a question: he was always going to be a big fish in the big pond of Rome, a latter-day Caesar of fashion. Before Valentino, haute couture meant Paris, where such great designers as Chanel and Balenciaga reigned. Still, Italy was developing a reputation for cheerful, attractive sportswear, its textile industry around Lake Como was rapidly developing, and the innate Italian sense for design and craftsmanship was poised to make a major fashion statement. Chic Roman designers such as Simonetta Fabiani and Roberto Capucci were busily dressing Rome's princesses as well as the movie stars of the Cinecittá studios, on the very edge of the Eternal City.

Valentino was born in 1932 in Voghera near Milan, where he studied before leaving for about a decade in Paris, working first with Jean Dessès, then Guy Laroche. He returned to Rome in 1959. His first collection in his own fashion house on the Via Condotti was an instant success, and among his first clients were Elizabeth Taylor, Rita Hayworth, Claudia Cardinale, and Italy's first lady Vittoria Leone. *Vogue* put his clothes on the cover, and soon he had shops in New York, Paris, Geneva, and London. His ready-to-wear shows became a fixture of Paris fashion

The tender yellow flowers of the rose 'Golden Wings' bloom next to the large blue perfumed spikes of a ceanothus (top) and the irises, which are ever-present in the Tuscan countryside (above). Opposite: One of the numerous statues in the garden is enhanced by a lustrous green curtain of ivy.

weeks, where the models were seen in big skirts, flamboyant ruffles, satin-edged flounces, elaborate embroidery, all with a dramatic use of black and red. He was the first couturier in Italy to achieve worldwide repute and the only one with a name that sounds noble. His reputation was certainly helped when he dressed Jackie Kennedy for her wedding with Aristotle Onassis. His achievements have always lived up to his reputation. Valentino today remains a fascinating fashion figure in a world where haute couture matters less and less. Today everything in Valentino's life returns us to the period when high fashion reigned and luxury was a habit. His country house La Vignola is about an hour's drive from Rome, and has all the joyous opulence of summer residences that fine gentlemen once built to escape from their weighty responsibilities at home. This aristocratic residence is on the border of Tuscany, and is one of those homes that only an Italian could dream up; it is what they call a villa. Once off the highway, Tuscany takes over, with endless vineyards and olive groves, golden fields of corn, and delicate green pastures that rustle like silk in the playful wind. All of Tuscany looks like a garden, and the meanest plot of land is arranged with a degree of refinement characteristic of the entire landscape. The sublime patchwork of planting was created with such artistry that you wonder whether the farmers are more concerned with how the land looks or what it yields. In the spring it is among the most refined agrarian cultures, and the fields overflow with blue irises under the countless olive trees. The countryside is so perfectly ordered that gardens often look disheveled by comparison. The garden of La Vignola, groaning under the weight of flowers and fruit, is no paragon of neatness—but this is by no means a criticism.

The ocher facade of the villa overlooks the square of the village, which is built on the side of a hill. Because the house nestles between two hills, the garden had to go on the hill in this crèche-shaped setting facing the village. The majestic flight of terraces that make their dramatic way up the slope are there by necessity. When Valentino found the house ten years ago, it was love at first sight. He bought a Baroque setting furnished with statues, busts, spheres, and ornamental vases, a summer house shaped like a pagoda, an eighteenth-century orangery, pools, pyramids, laurel copses, niches made of pebble mosaics, a *rocaille* grotto, and an enormous quantity of period Tuscan earthenware pots, each one an object of enormous interest in itself.

Preceding pages: The long white cluster of wisteria flowers follows the contours of a chalk wall.
Above: In the Tuscan spring, horse chestnuts bloom at the same time as citrus fruit cultivated in pots, which have already begun to show their blossoms.
Opposite, above: The potted lemons are in fruit throughout the summer in front of the house.
Opposite, below: The garden also includes an arena for the purebred Arabian horses given to Valentino by the king of Spain.

Since all elements were already in place, all the designer had to do when he became the owner was to begin restoration. Valentino had the help of landscape artist Paolo Pejrone, who is credited with drawing the garden out of its lethargy while preserving that air of abandon that goes so well with the Baroque. One of his tactics was to leave the rock garden in a somewhat dilapidated state: the statues are so overgrown with lichen and moss that the marks of time look positively artistic. "There was no question of changing anything," Valentino says. It would have been unthinkable to make an English or Japanese garden in so Baroque a setting. "Which doesn't mean that I like only Baroque gardens, far from it," he adds. By temperament he does tend to favor a certain exuberance of shape and color, but he insists that he has no preconceived ideas.

If what he likes is exuberance, then La Vignola is the answer to Valentino's prayers. "It's a sort of *commedia dell'arte* acted out in full sunshine," he says, pointing out the harlequinade of vivid colors created by the citrus fruits in the almost black foliage of the orange and lemon trees.

"All these flowers are very unruly, you know, even a bit crazy sometimes. The outrageous way they behave, you'd think they were doing it deliberately to annoy the gardener." The pruned box borders that were intended to contain the flowers have become obstacles that the flowers are determined to overcome. "I like the paradox expressed by this profusion of the most exquisite delicacy," says an ecstatic Valentino. "The gracefulness of a rose as it loses its petals is something that appeals to my idea of fashion. It's an extremely feminine form of abandon. It makes you feel the same as when mousseline slips off a woman's shoulder or reveals her breast beneath the thin material. For me, there is something eternally feminine about a mode of seduction that reveals a certain fragility in the midst of opulence."

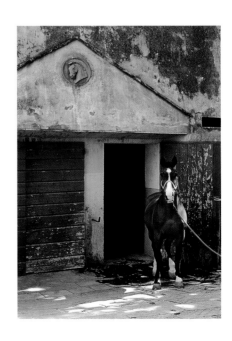

Alleys either paved or lined with earthenware bricks criss-cross the lawn in front of the villa, reminding one of the partitioned designs typical of Italian Renaissance gardens. There is nothing geometric about the overall design, though, thanks to the profusion of plants that char-

Above: *The entrance
to the house is a model
of sophistication, which is
reflected in the choice
of pottery, the
ornamentation of the
door, and the bust set
above it.*
Opposite: *In this
Baroque garden, sober
arrangements are
sometimes effective. This
simple but enormous oil
pot is placed at the foot
of a purple wisteria.*
Following pages:
*Two striking views of the
Tuscan hillside from one
of the many terraces in
the garden. In the
foreground of the first
(left), a delicate, semi-
double rose finds the
perfect support in a simple
wooden fence. The second
view (right) is framed by
the imposing dark green
mass of two tapering
cypress trees, so typical of
this countryside.*

acterizes La Vignola; among these are avalanches of roses, guelder roses (*Viburnum opulus*) and syringa (*Lilac*). When the weather turns fine the potted orange and box trees resume their rightful place at the corners of the borders. They upset the original layout, but they also mix a touch of Neoclassicism in with the Baroque. Nature makes sure everything hangs together: for example, cascading clusters of tight, white wisteria tumble down one of the supporting walls that retain the terraces, and also pour down the sides of the *rocaille* grotto, filling the air there with a freshness that seems a preparation for the humidity inside.

From here a path leads to an orangery shrouded in vines and roses. Four busts of women rise from the vegetation as if looking for passersby on the roof. La Vignola is characterized by an excess of decoration that is as surprising as it is stunning. The espaliered garden contributes to this effect by making the visitor lose all sense of height. "Each bedroom opens on to a terrace," explains the couturier, proud to share nature with his guests. Indeed, there is a tradition of hospitality in this house. Throughout, immense bouquets remind you of the abundance you will find at the dinner table, and all the fruit and vegetables are homegrown. "People are often surprised at how extraordinarily good they taste," remarks Valentino, who eats nothing but vegetables and pasta.

The path continues past the house and makes its way to the top of the hill. Rather steep, it is bordered by a row of cypress trees that make it that much grander. Animals are king at here, and are particularly royal at the top of the hill. There, tucked away at the end of a field of olive trees are the stables that Valentino built to house the Arab thorough-breds that were a gift from the King of Spain. It's quite odd to suddenly find oneself in a field in the countryside, surrounded by wildflowers, when just five minutes before you were immersed in the Baroque. With Tuscany in the background, this seems just one more theatrical effect of the spirit of the period.

Nicole de Vésian

Abundance

and Austerity

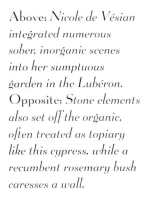

Above: *Nicole de Vésian integrated numerous sober, inorganic scenes into her sumptuous garden in the Lubéron.*
Opposite: *Stone elements also set off the organic, often treated as topiary like this cypress, while a recumbent rosemary bush caresses a wall.*

"Each time I go back there, I can feel her spiritual power," says Issey Miyake about the garden that Nicole de Vésian left behind in Bonnieux, a little village in the south of France. De Vésian was head of fashion at Hermès for many years, an influential member of the Fashion Group, and one of the pioneering women designers who revolutionized our daily lives. Before them, the term "fashion designer" did not exist. Miyake is not alone in the strength of his reaction. In fact, rarely does a garden arouse such powerful emotions. Jean-Louis Dumas of Hermès remembers her as follows: "Nicole de Vésian was chic personified. Her look, her profile, her allure, creations, and marriage of leather and flannel, in fact everything she designed immediately took on a cachet of elegance. During the many years she worked at Hermès, her studio was located under the eaves of 26 Rue du Faubourg St. Honoré, our headquarters. There was an access door to the terrace at number 24, and Nicole was my accomplice in planting the garden there. Today, the magnolia, bouquets of rosemary, the September roses, and the apple trees dripping with fruit perpetuate the memory of her presence. Before, up there were two staircases embellished with frolicking putti: 'That is why,' said Nicole, 'we must put stones in their garden.' This grand lady

followed this advice at Bonnieux, where, under her magic fingers, there grew up a veritable paradise of the meridional plants and stones of the Lubéron. I can still see her notes on my desk, written on kraft paper. Her ideas were always set out in a few words, based on a concept explained by a triangle. This basic approach, this well-balanced thought was solidly balanced by the three points of the triangle: light, appropriate, and elegant, adjectives that fit Vésian as well as a glove."

Surveying the terraces facing the hills of the Lubéron, the word harmony takes on an almost cosmic sense that gives new depth to the idea of the environment. If de Vésian's garden blends with the surrounding *garrigue,* the local name for the wild-herb undergrowth of Provence, it also seems at one with earthly and spiritual forces. The garden seems to respond to signals that echo off the cypress trees, reuniting the sky, earth, rocks, and plants in a subtle but perfect osmosis. The view extends over wave upon wave of rolling hills all the way to the horizon, endlessly changing color with the light. De Vésian knew how to make the most of

this view, and those hills are certainly the shapes she had in mind when she started clipping the aromatic herbs that make up the garden. At first they appear to be a gray mass of rounded bumps that could be either mineral or vegetable. This rather Japanese effect is reinforced by gray rocks that look like sponges lurking under monochrome borders.

The garden can only be reached through the house, which literally hangs off the side of a rock and is the last building in a village that hurtles down a stony hillside. The ground is lined with pebbles from the bed of the Durance River, the vaulting is of solid stone, and the reinforcements are troglodytic. There are more stones than flowers, and although that comes as no surprise, the severity is startling, especially considering that this was the home of a Parisian lady of fashion. But the house and garden draw an accurate picture of the kind of woman de Vésian was. A range of somber, understated tones is enriched by the touches of ocher and off-white added by the fountain, mill stone, funeral stele, balusters, spheres, and a collection of stone blocks scattered throughout. There is

Opposite, above: A river of lavender runs between the gold of deciduous trees and the dark green of cypress. Opposite, below: The evergreens are sometimes formed into parasols. Above: The view extends endlessly over the gentle wooded hills that reflect the numerous hillocks of lavender, santolina, teucrium, cineraria, and box in the garden. Following pages: On a paved terrace, masses of box trimmed into rounded cushions seem posed like pawns on a chessboard. The symmetry of the group is accentuated by the presence of four columns of cypress, trimmed identically, on either side of a stone bench.

a great range of greens, from silvery and verdigris to powdery, faded, almost bleached, dusty green. Nature is the greatest colorist there is, and what rare touches of color there are here stand out against this spare canvas: the red bark of an arbutus or the white flowers of a rose bush, pink cistus flowers, or the occasional burst of iris that illuminates a low wall of loose stones in the spring.

When Nicole de Vésian came to Bonnieux she had just turned seventy and, incredibly, knew nothing about gardening. She had always said that she owed her imagination to her wartime childhood, when one had to invent whatever one needed, which, during the war, meant nearly everything. So at the close of a very full professional life she found herself drawn to a place that required some invention on her part. Judging from the aridity of her garden, which is far from austere, she was right to say, "It isn't a rich person's garden." Among the treasures she collected on her walks were strangely shaped stones, gnarled bits of tree trunks, and driftwood. Her garden was also a refuge for plants that professional gardeners had long given up on.

De Vésian was self-educated by vocation and choice. She learned by watching—noticing which plants grew wild in the *garrigue*, then growing those plants at home. She concentrated on plants that thrive in a dry climate: rosemary, box, santolina, sage, lavender (sometimes cut so close as to be unrecognizable), cineraria, and teucrium (cat thyme). Most are aromatics, and their fragrances fill the air. Rather rugged flora, some might say, but de Vésian achieved wonderful effects with her shears, and today these little bushes nestling softly together look like waves rolling along the terraces.

Every morning de Vésian would inspect the bushes and make adjustments with her nail scissors. Even the cypresses, which are usually truncated and beveled, got a haircut. When asked about her gardening secrets, she would say, "a touch of sheep dung in the spring." Although it sounds strange, there is apparently no better way to protect plants from drought. It makes them tough enough to survive the lack of water all year, even in the summer heat.

De Vésian's garden is at once dreamlike and minimalist, a highly personal creation that many have since tried to copy. It started a fashion in Provence, and one now finds versions of it all over the world, from New Zealand to New Hampshire. Nature was an endless source of inspiration for de Vésian's fertile imagination. Even natural

Against a row of box trimmed into perfect spheres, the flowering of the lavender seems more disheveled than ever and provides a remarkable contrast of volume and color.

disasters fed her creativity. She once transformed a wall that had collapsed in torrential rain into a rock garden. But terms like rock garden and topiary, although perfectly correct, are not accurate descriptions of what she created. Her meandering, ultra-feminine sensitivity found new ways to express classical shapes. She despised symmetry, shunned the path of least resistance, and apparently cared little for the perpendicular.

All those who knew de Vésian towards the end of her life remember her extraordinary vitality and devastating chic. She would pace the hillside tirelessly, armed with her leather-bound walking stick from Hermès. Only after her eightieth birthday did the steepest paths become a prob-

lem. The narrow steps from one terrace to another increased the chances of a fall, and the uneven ground made walking extremely hazardous. Her solution was to create another garden, this time in a flatter place at the top of the hill, but death interrupted her.

Today de Vésian's garden is cared for by Judith Pillsbury, a woman originally from California who now lives mostly in Paris. De Vésian handpicked her to take care of the garden, knowing that she would not only need to maintain it, but would also have to oversee changes, as its creator had, in the spirit of the place. Pillsbury has added several plants and done some stone work, but like de Vésian she is devoted to the process of developing the wealth of natural beauty.

A theatrical scene organizes itself around this beautiful stone sphere, set off by the protruding and imposing masses of box and the columns of cypress in the back, as well as by the low cushions of spindle tree and rosemary in the foreground.

Acknowledgments

I would like to warmly thank all the owners and gardeners who so courteously and generously opened the doors to their gardens, as well as Bertrand and my children, who put up with the ever changing weather conditions which made for my constant change of plans.

Claire de Virieu

I would like to express my special gratitude to Marie-Claire Pauwels, director of *Madame Figaro*, without whose support this book would not have been possible.

For their invaluable support and patience, I also thank Frédéric Basset, Jérôme Bartau, Bruno Chambelland, Hélène Chauvet, Casimir Cheuvreux, Madison Cox, Kevin Doyle, Gaëlle de Gasquet, Isabel Harvie-Watt, Gaëlle Le Targat, Danièle Leclercq, Maryline Lops, Janine Pagenel, Chessy Reiner, François de Riqlès, Joseph Rokacz, Brigitte Vermillet, Bertrand de Virieu, Isabella Visconti, and Charlotte von Zeppelin.

I should also like to thank many people who gave me their help, particularly Nevil Ablitt, Beatrice Barro, Louis Benech, Olivia Berghauer, Isabella Capeche, Vincent Debiar, Yasmina Den Mati, Dominique Deroche, Olivier Fretté, Quito Fierro, Joël Fournier, Marchese di San Giuliano, Barbara Goddard, Anne Kerbec, Thaddée Klossowski de Rola, Camille Müller, Emanuela Notarbartolo di Sciara, Ruth Obadia, Umberto Pasti, Judith Pillsbury, Annette de la Renta, Jean-François Ricat, Arielle Ricaud-Barsi, Carlos Souza, Hubert de Vésian.

I would also like to thank Marike Gauthier, Sabine Greenberg and Owen Dugan for their editing, and Marc Walter for his design.

Finally, a great number of the photographs were made possible thanks to the efficiency of Air France and Europcar.

César Garçon

Printed and bound in Italy
by Artegrafica, Verona
Color separation by Planète Graphique